Character Design Workbook:
Pocket Edition

ISBN: 9798565544022
Character Development Workbook: Pocket Edition
Copyright:2020
Care Halverson
INKmagine and Create

Story:	Role: MC, 2nd MC, 3rd MC, protagonist, antagonist, love interest, side kick, hapless bystander, other:
Book:	
Series:	Archetype: Tip: people have multiple facets. We don't pop out of molds.
Genre:	Primary Antagonist:

Name:
Tip: vary in first letter and length to limit confusion.

Age:

Eye Color:

Meaning:

DOB:

Hair Color:

Alias:

Height:

Hair Type:

Title:

Weight:

Hair Style:

Gender:

Build:

Skin Color:

Sexuality:

Blood Type:

Skin Tone:

Species:

Dominant Hand:

Voice:

Race:
Heritage born with.

Ethnicity:
Ethnicity is learned cultural behaviors.

Accent:
Tip: use with light touch.

Relationship Status:

Financial Status:

Social Class:

Identifying Features: injuries, scars, prosthetic, birthmarks, freckles, piercings, tattoos, alien features, biotech, scales, fangs, horns, ears, glasses, contacts, dimples, etc

Likes/Dislikes, Comforts/Fears, Strength/Weakness, Habits/Ticks

Character Traits

Tip: We are each a messy conflicted ball of contradictions. How can their own traits clash and force them to choose between two parts of themselves?

Introvert/Extrovert
Sarcastic/Quiet
Thinker/Feeler
Judger/Perceiver
Sensing/Intuition
Calm/Excitable
Timid/Outgoing
Left Brain/Right Brain
Pessimist/Optimist/Realist
Motivated/Unmotivated
Controlled/Impulsive
Humble/Egotistical
Polite/Rude
A-B-O
Prioritizes/Procrastinates
Indoors/Outdoors
Efficient/Inefficient
Agile/Clumsy/Strong
Fight/Flight
Mischievous/Serious
Mature/Immature
Lazy/Hardworking
Predator/Prey
Common-Sense/Book-smarts
Private/TMI

Childish/Mature
Kind/Cruel/Uncaring
Laidback/High-strung
Cautious/Reckless
Leader/Follower
Loyal/Disloyal
Suspicious/Trusting
Mouth-filter/No-mouth-filter
Patient/Impatient
Intelligent/Average/Dumb-as-a-rock
Professional/Unprofessional
Formal/Informal
Quiet/Loud
Dominant/Submissive
Early/Late/On-Time
Athletic/Sedentary
Frivolous/Conservative
Routine/Spontaneity
Competitive/Passive
Self-blame/Blames-others
Logical/Emotional
Dedicated/Gives up
Flash Decisions/Contemplates
Wise/Foolish
Stubborn/Docile

Honest/Dishonest
Decisive/Indecisive
Forgiving/Grudges
Generous/Stingy
Warm/Cold
Grounded/Flighty
Reliable/Unreliable
Open/Secretive
Direct/Cautious/Daredevil
Dependent/Independent
Watcher/Participant
Night/Day
City/Country
Words/Fists
Neat/Messy
Focused/Distracted
Imaginative/Academic
Frugal/Wasteful
Flexible/Inflexible
Sweet/Sour/Bitter
Organized/Disorganized
Calm/Hot-tempered
Close/Long/Middle
Listens/Bullheaded
Generous/Selfish

Motivations: Wants or Needs: these often conflict.

_____
_____
_____
_____

What conflicts stand in the way?

_____
_____
_____

Notes:

_____
_____
_____
_____
_____

Story:	Role: MC, 2nd MC, 3rd MC, protagonist, antagonist, love interest, side kick, hapless bystander, other:
Book:	
Series:	Archetype: Tip: people have multiple facets. We don't pop out of molds.
Genre:	Primary Antagonist:

Name:
Tip: vary in first letter and length to limit confusion.

Age:

Eye Color:

Meaning:

DOB:

Hair Color:

Alias:

Height:

Hair Type:

Title:

Weight:

Hair Style:

Gender:

Build:

Skin Color:

Sexuality:

Blood Type:

Skin Tone:

Species:

Dominant Hand:

Voice:

Race:

Heritage born with.

Ethnicity:

Ethnicity is learned cultural behaviors.

Accent:

Tip: use with light touch.

Relationship Status:

Financial Status:

Social Class:

Identifying Features: injuries, scars, prosthetic, birthmarks, freckles, piercings, tattoos, alien features, biotech, scales, fangs, horns, ears, glasses, contacts, dimples, etc

Likes/Dislikes, Comforts/Fears, Strength/Weakness, Habits/Ticks

Character Traits

Tip: We are each a messy conflicted ball of contradictions. How can their own traits clash and force them to choose between two parts of themselves?

Introvert/Extrovert	Childish/Mature	Honest/Dishonest
Sarcastic/Quiet	Kind/Cruel/Uncaring	Decisive/Indecisive
Thinker/Feeler	Laidback/High-strung	Forgiving/Grudges
Judger/Perceiver	Cautious/Reckless	Generous/Stingy
Sensing/Intuition	Leader/Follower	Warm/Cold
Calm/Excitable	Loyal/Disloyal	Grounded/Flighty
Timid/Outgoing	Suspicious/Trusting	Reliable/Unreliable
Left Brain/Right Brain	Mouth-filter/No-mouth-filter	Open/Secretive
Pessimist/Optimist/Realist	Patient/Impatient	Direct/Cautious/Daredevil
Motivated/Unmotivated	Intelligent/Average/Dumb-as-	Dependent/Independent
Controlled/Impulsive	a-rock	Watcher/Participant
Humble/Egotistical	Professional/Unprofessional	Night/Day
Polite/Rude	Formal/Informal	City/Country
A-B-O	Quiet/Loud	Words/Fists
Prioritizes/Procrastinates	Dominant/Submissive	Neat/Messy
Indoors/Outdoors	Early/Late/On-Time	Focused/Distracted
Efficient/Inefficient	Athletic/Sedentary	Imaginative/Academic
Agile/Clumsy/Strong	Frivolous/Conservative	Frugal/Wasteful
Fight/Flight	Routine/Spontaneity	Flexible/Inflexible
Mischievous/Serious	Competitive/Passive	Sweet/Sour/Bitter
Mature/Immature	Self-blame/Blames-others	Organized/Disorganized
Lazy/Hardworking	Logical/Emotional	Calm/Hot-tempered
Predator/Prey	Dedicated/Gives up	Close/Long/Middle
Common-Sense/Book-	Flash Decisions/Contemplates	Listens/Bullheaded
smarts	Wise/Foolish	Generous/Selfish
Private/TMI	Stubborn/Docile	

Motivations: Wants or Needs: these often conflict.

_____
_____
_____
_____

What conflicts stand in the way?

_____
_____
_____

Notes:

_____
_____
_____
_____
_____

Story:	Role: MC, 2nd MC, 3rd MC, protagonist, antagonist, love interest, side kick, hapless bystander, other:
Book:	
Series:	Archetype: Tip: people have multiple facets. We don't pop out of molds.
Genre:	Primary Antagonist:

Name:
Tip: vary in first letter and length to limit confusion.

Age:

Eye Color:

Meaning:

DOB:

Hair Color:

Alias:

Height:

Hair Type:

Title:

Weight:

Hair Style:

Gender:

Build:

Skin Color:

Sexuality:

Blood Type:

Skin Tone:

Species:

Dominant Hand:

Voice:

Race:

Heritage born with.

Ethnicity:

Ethnicity is learned cultural behaviors.

Accent:

Tip: use with light touch.

Relationship Status:

Financial Status:

Social Class:

Identifying Features: injuries, scars, prosthetic, birthmarks, freckles, piercings, tattoos, alien features, biotech, scales, fangs, horns, ears, glasses, contacts, dimples, etc

Likes/Dislikes, Comforts/Fears, Strength/Weakness, Habits/Ticks

Character Traits

Tip: We are each a messy conflicted ball of contradictions. How can their own traits clash and force them to choose between two parts of themselves?

Introvert/Extrovert
Sarcastic/Quiet
Thinker/Feeler
Judger/Perceiver
Sensing/Intuition
Calm/Excitable
Timid/Outgoing
Left Brain/Right Brain
Pessimist/Optimist/Realist
Motivated/Unmotivated
Controlled/Impulsive
Humble/Egotistical
Polite/Rude
A-B-O
Prioritizes/Procrastinates
Indoors/Outdoors
Efficient/Inefficient
Agile/Clumsy/Strong
Fight/Flight
Mischievous/Serious
Mature/Immature
Lazy/Hardworking
Predator/Prey
Common-Sense/Book-smarts
Private/TMI

Childish/Mature
Kind/Cruel/Uncaring
Laidback/High-strung
Cautious/Reckless
Leader/Follower
Loyal/Disloyal
Suspicious/Trusting
Mouth-filter/No-mouth-filter
Patient/Impatient
Intelligent/Average/Dumb-as-a-rock
Professional/Unprofessional
Formal/Informal
Quiet/Loud
Dominant/Submissive
Early/Late/On-Time
Athletic/Sedentary
Frivolous/Conservative
Routine/Spontaneity
Competitive/Passive
Self-blame/Blames-others
Logical/Emotional
Dedicated/Gives up
Flash Decisions/Contemplates
Wise/Foolish
Stubborn/Docile

Honest/Dishonest
Decisive/Indecisive
Forgiving/Grudges
Generous/Stingy
Warm/Cold
Grounded/Flighty
Reliable/Unreliable
Open/Secretive
Direct/Cautious/Daredevil
Dependent/Independent
Watcher/Participant
Night/Day
City/Country
Words/Fists
Neat/Messy
Focused/Distracted
Imaginative/Academic
Frugal/Wasteful
Flexible/Inflexible
Sweet/Sour/Bitter
Organized/Disorganized
Calm/Hot-tempered
Close/Long/Middle
Listens/Bullheaded
Generous/Selfish

Motivations: Wants or Needs: these often conflict.

_____
_____
_____
_____

What conflicts stand in the way?

_____
_____
_____

Notes:

_____
_____
_____
_____
_____

Story:	Role: MC, 2nd MC, 3rd MC, protagonist, antagonist, love interest, side kick, hapless bystander, other:
Book:	
Series:	Archetype: Tip: people have multiple facets. We don't pop out of molds.
Genre:	Primary Antagonist:

Name:
Tip: vary in first letter and length to limit confusion.

Age:

Eye Color:

Meaning:

DOB:

Hair Color:

Alias:

Height:

Hair Type:

Title:

Weight:

Hair Style:

Gender:

Build:

Skin Color:

Sexuality:

Blood Type:

Skin Tone:

Species:

Dominant Hand:

Voice:

Race:

Heritage born with.

Ethnicity:
Ethnicity is learned cultural behaviors.

Accent:
Tip: use with light touch.

Relationship Status:

Financial Status:

Social Class:

Identifying Features: injuries, scars, prosthetic, birthmarks, freckles, piercings, tattoos, alien features, biotech, scales, fangs, horns, ears, glasses, contacts, dimples, etc

Likes/Dislikes, Comforts/Fears, Strength/Weakness, Habits/Ticks

Character Traits

Tip: We are each a messy conflicted ball of contradictions. How can their own traits clash and force them to choose between two parts of themselves?

Introvert/Extrovert
Sarcastic/Quiet
Thinker/Feeler
Judger/Perceiver
Sensing/Intuition
Calm/Excitable
Timid/Outgoing
Left Brain/Right Brain
Pessimist/Optimist/Realist
Motivated/Unmotivated
Controlled/Impulsive
Humble/Egotistical
Polite/Rude
A-B-O
Prioritizes/Procrastinates
Indoors/Outdoors
Efficient/Inefficient
Agile/Clumsy/Strong
Fight/Flight
Mischievous/Serious
Mature/Immature
Lazy/Hardworking
Predator/Prey
Common-Sense/Book-smarts
Private/TMI

Childish/Mature
Kind/Cruel/Uncaring
Laidback/High-strung
Cautious/Reckless
Leader/Follower
Loyal/Disloyal
Suspicious/Trusting
Mouth-filter/No-mouth-filter
Patient/Impatient
Intelligent/Average/Dumb-as-a-rock
Professional/Unprofessional
Formal/Informal
Quiet/Loud
Dominant/Submissive
Early/Late/On-Time
Athletic/Sedentary
Frivolous/Conservative
Routine/Spontaneity
Competitive/Passive
Self-blame/Blames-others
Logical/Emotional
Dedicated/Gives up
Flash Decisions/Contemplates
Wise/Foolish
Stubborn/Docile

Honest/Dishonest
Decisive/Indecisive
Forgiving/Grudges
Generous/Stingy
Warm/Cold
Grounded/Flighty
Reliable/Unreliable
Open/Secretive
Direct/Cautious/Daredevil
Dependent/Independent
Watcher/Participant
Night/Day
City/Country
Words/Fists
Neat/Messy
Focused/Distracted
Imaginative/Academic
Frugal/Wasteful
Flexible/Inflexible
Sweet/Sour/Bitter
Organized/Disorganized
Calm/Hot-tempered
Close/Long/Middle
Listens/Bullheaded
Generous/Selfish

Motivations: Wants or Needs: these often conflict.

_____
_____
_____
_____

What conflicts stand in the way?

_____
_____
_____

Notes:

_____
_____
_____
_____
_____

Story:	Role: MC, 2nd MC, 3rd MC, protagonist, antagonist, love interest, side kick, hapless bystander, other:
Book:	
Series:	Archetype: Tip: people have multiple facets. We don't pop out of molds.
Genre:	Primary Antagonist:

Name:
Tip: vary in first letter and length to limit confusion.

Age:

Eye Color:

Meaning:

DOB:

Hair Color:

Alias:

Height:

Hair Type:

Title:

Weight:

Hair Style:

Gender:

Build:

Skin Color:

Sexuality:

Blood Type:

Skin Tone:

Species:

Dominant Hand:

Voice:

Race:

Heritage born with.

Ethnicity:

Ethnicity is learned cultural behaviors.

Accent:

Tip: use with light touch.

Relationship Status:

Financial Status:

Social Class:

Identifying Features: injuries, scars, prosthetic, birthmarks, freckles, piercings, tattoos, alien features, biotech, scales, fangs, horns, ears, glasses, contacts, dimples, etc

Likes/Dislikes, Comforts/Fears, Strength/Weakness, Habits/Ticks

Character Traits

Tip: We are each a messy conflicted ball of contradictions. How can their own traits clash and force them to choose between two parts of themselves?

Introvert/Extrovert	Childish/Mature	Honest/Dishonest
Sarcastic/Quiet	Kind/Cruel/Uncaring	Decisive/Indecisive
Thinker/Feeler	Laidback/High-strung	Forgiving/Grudges
Judger/Perceiver	Cautious/Reckless	Generous/Stingy
Sensing/Intuition	Leader/Follower	Warm/Cold
Calm/Excitable	Loyal/Disloyal	Grounded/Flighty
Timid/Outgoing	Suspicious/Trusting	Reliable/Unreliable
Left Brain/Right Brain	Mouth-filter/No-mouth-filter	Open/Secretive
Pessimist/Optimist/Realist	Patient/Impatient	Direct/Cautious/Daredevil
Motivated/Unmotivated	Intelligent/Average/Dumb-as-	Dependent/Independent
Controlled/Impulsive	a-rock	Watcher/Participant
Humble/Egotistical	Professional/Unprofessional	Night/Day
Polite/Rude	Formal/Informal	City/Country
A-B-O	Quiet/Loud	Words/Fists
Prioritizes/Procrastinates	Dominant/Submissive	Neat/Messy
Indoors/Outdoors	Early/Late/On-Time	Focused/Distracted
Efficient/Inefficient	Athletic/Sedentary	Imaginative/Academic
Agile/Clumsy/Strong	Frivolous/Conservative	Frugal/Wasteful
Fight/Flight	Routine/Spontaneity	Flexible/Inflexible
Mischievous/Serious	Competitive/Passive	Sweet/Sour/Bitter
Mature/Immature	Self-blame/Blames-others	Organized/Disorganized
Lazy/Hardworking	Logical/Emotional	Calm/Hot-tempered
Predator/Prey	Dedicated/Gives up	Close/Long/Middle
Common-Sense/Book-	Flash Decisions/Contemplates	Listens/Bullheaded
smarts	Wise/Foolish	Generous/Selfish
Private/TMI	Stubborn/Docile	

Motivations: Wants or Needs: these often conflict.

_____

_____

_____

_____

What conflicts stand in the way?

_____

_____

_____

Notes:

_____

_____

_____

_____

_____

Story:	Role: MC, 2nd MC, 3rd MC, protagonist, antagonist, love interest, side kick, hapless bystander, other:
Book:	
Series:	Archetype: Tip: people have multiple facets. We don't pop out of molds.
Genre:	Primary Antagonist:

Name:
Tip: vary in first letter and length to limit confusion.

Age:

Eye Color:

Meaning:

DOB:

Hair Color:

Alias:

Height:

Hair Type:

Title:

Weight:

Hair Style:

Gender:

Build:

Skin Color:

Sexuality:

Blood Type:

Skin Tone:

Species:

Dominant Hand:

Voice:

Race:
Heritage born with.

Ethnicity:
Ethnicity is learned cultural behaviors.

Accent:
Tip: use with light touch.

Relationship Status:

Financial Status:

Social Class:

Identifying Features: injuries, scars, prosthetic, birthmarks, freckles, piercings, tattoos, alien features, biotech, scales, fangs, horns, ears, glasses, contacts, dimples, etc

Likes/Dislikes, Comforts/Fears, Strength/Weakness, Habits/Ticks

Character Traits

Tip: We are each a messy conflicted ball of contradictions. How can their own traits clash and force them to choose between two parts of themselves?

Introvert/Extrovert	Childish/Mature	Honest/Dishonest
Sarcastic/Quiet	Kind/Cruel/Uncaring	Decisive/Indecisive
Thinker/Feeler	Laidback/High-strung	Forgiving/Grudges
Judger/Perceiver	Cautious/Reckless	Generous/Stingy
Sensing/Intuition	Leader/Follower	Warm/Cold
Calm/Excitable	Loyal/Disloyal	Grounded/Flighty
Timid/Outgoing	Suspicious/Trusting	Reliable/Unreliable
Left Brain/Right Brain	Mouth-filter/No-mouth-filter	Open/Secretive
Pessimist/Optimist/Realist	Patient/Impatient	Direct/Cautious/Daredevil
Motivated/Unmotivated	Intelligent/Average/Dumb-as-a-rock	Dependent/Independent
Controlled/Impulsive	a-rock	Watcher/Participant
Humble/Egotistical	Professional/Unprofessional	Night/Day
Polite/Rude	Formal/Informal	City/Country
A-B-O	Quiet/Loud	Words/Fists
Prioritizes/Procrastinates	Dominant/Submissive	Neat/Messy
Indoors/Outdoors	Early/Late/On-Time	Focused/Distracted
Efficient/Inefficient	Athletic/Sedentary	Imaginative/Academic
Agile/Clumsy/Strong	Frivolous/Conservative	Frugal/Wasteful
Fight/Flight	Routine/Spontaneity	Flexible/Inflexible
Mischievous/Serious	Competitive/Passive	Sweet/Sour/Bitter
Mature/Immature	Self-blame/Blames-others	Organized/Disorganized
Lazy/Hardworking	Logical/Emotional	Calm/Hot-tempered
Predator/Prey	Dedicated/Gives up	Close/Long/Middle
Common-Sense/Book-smarts	Flash Decisions/Contemplates	Listens/Bullheaded
smarts	Wise/Foolish	Generous/Selfish
Private/TMI	Stubborn/Docile	

Motivations: Wants or Needs: these often conflict.

_____
_____
_____
_____

What conflicts stand in the way?

_____
_____
_____

Notes:

_____
_____
_____
_____
_____

Story:	Role: MC, 2nd MC, 3rd MC, protagonist, antagonist, love interest, side kick, hapless bystander, other:
Book:	
Series:	Archetype: Tip: people have multiple facets. We don't pop out of molds.
Genre:	Primary Antagonist:

Name:
Tip: vary in first letter and length to limit confusion.

Age:

Eye Color:

Meaning:

DOB:

Hair Color:

Alias:

Height:

Hair Type:

Title:

Weight:

Hair Style:

Gender:

Build:

Skin Color:

Sexuality:

Blood Type:

Skin Tone:

Species:

Dominant Hand:

Voice:

Race:
Heritage born with.

Ethnicity:
Ethnicity is learned cultural behaviors.

Accent:
Tip: use with light touch.

Relationship Status:

Financial Status:

Social Class:

Identifying Features: injuries, scars, prosthetic, birthmarks, freckles, piercings, tattoos, alien features, biotech, scales, fangs, horns, ears, glasses, contacts, dimples, etc

Likes/Dislikes, Comforts/Fears, Strength/Weakness, Habits/Ticks

Character Traits

Tip: We are each a messy conflicted ball of contradictions. How can their own traits clash and force them to choose between two parts of themselves?

Introvert/Extrovert
Sarcastic/Quiet
Thinker/Feeler
Judger/Perceiver
Sensing/Intuition
Calm/Excitable
Timid/Outgoing
Left Brain/Right Brain
Pessimist/Optimist/Realist
Motivated/Unmotivated
Controlled/Impulsive
Humble/Egotistical
Polite/Rude
A-B-O
Prioritizes/Procrastinates
Indoors/Outdoors
Efficient/Inefficient
Agile/Clumsy/Strong
Fight/Flight
Mischievous/Serious
Mature/Immature
Lazy/Hardworking
Predator/Prey
Common-Sense/Book-smarts
Private/TMI

Childish/Mature
Kind/Cruel/Uncaring
Laidback/High-strung
Cautious/Reckless
Leader/Follower
Loyal/Disloyal
Suspicious/Trusting
Mouth-filter/No-mouth-filter
Patient/Impatient
Intelligent/Average/Dumb-as-a-rock
Professional/Unprofessional
Formal/Informal
Quiet/Loud
Dominant/Submissive
Early/Late/On-Time
Athletic/Sedentary
Frivolous/Conservative
Routine/Spontaneity
Competitive/Passive
Self-blame/Blames-others
Logical/Emotional
Dedicated/Gives up
Flash Decisions/Contemplates
Wise/Foolish
Stubborn/Docile

Honest/Dishonest
Decisive/Indecisive
Forgiving/Grudges
Generous/Stingy
Warm/Cold
Grounded/Flighty
Reliable/Unreliable
Open/Secretive
Direct/Cautious/Daredevil
Dependent/Independent
Watcher/Participant
Night/Day
City/Country
Words/Fists
Neat/Messy
Focused/Distracted
Imaginative/Academic
Frugal/Wasteful
Flexible/Inflexible
Sweet/Sour/Bitter
Organized/Disorganized
Calm/Hot-tempered
Close/Long/Middle
Listens/Bullheaded
Generous/Selfish

Motivations: Wants or Needs: these often conflict.

_____
_____
_____
_____

What conflicts stand in the way?

_____
_____
_____

Notes:

_____
_____
_____
_____
_____

Story:	Role: MC, 2nd MC, 3rd MC, protagonist, antagonist, love interest, side kick, hapless bystander, other:
Book:	
Series:	Archetype: Tip: people have multiple facets. We don't pop out of molds.
Genre:	Primary Antagonist:

Name:
Tip: vary in first letter and length to limit confusion.

Age:

Eye Color:

Meaning:

DOB:

Hair Color:

Alias:

Height:

Hair Type:

Title:

Weight:

Hair Style:

Gender:

Build:

Skin Color:

Sexuality:

Blood Type:

Skin Tone:

Species: .

Dominant Hand:

Voice:

Race:
Heritage born with.

Ethnicity:
Ethnicity is learned cultural behaviors.

Accent:
Tip: use with light touch.

Relationship Status:

Financial Status:

Social Class:

Identifying Features: injuries, scars, prosthetic, birthmarks, freckles, piercings, tattoos, alien features, biotech, scales, fangs, horns, ears, glasses, contacts, dimples, etc

Likes/Dislikes, Comforts/Fears, Strength/Weakness, Habits/Ticks

Character Traits

Tip: We are each a messy conflicted ball of contradictions. How can their own traits clash and force them to choose between two parts of themselves?

Introvert/Extrovert
Sarcastic/Quiet
Thinker/Feeler
Judger/Perceiver
Sensing/Intuition
Calm/Excitable
Timid/Outgoing
Left Brain/Right Brain
Pessimist/Optimist/Realist
Motivated/Unmotivated
Controlled/Impulsive
Humble/Egotistical
Polite/Rude
A-B-O
Prioritizes/Procrastinates
Indoors/Outdoors
Efficient/Inefficient
Agile/Clumsy/Strong
Fight/Flight
Mischievous/Serious
Mature/Immature
Lazy/Hardworking
Predator/Prey
Common-Sense/Book-smarts
Private/TMI

Childish/Mature
Kind/Cruel/Uncaring
Laidback/High-strung
Cautious/Reckless
Leader/Follower
Loyal/Disloyal
Suspicious/Trusting
Mouth-filter/No-mouth-filter
Patient/Impatient
Intelligent/Average/Dumb-as-a-rock
Professional/Unprofessional
Formal/Informal
Quiet/Loud
Dominant/Submissive
Early/Late/On-Time
Athletic/Sedentary
Frivolous/Conservative
Routine/Spontaneity
Competitive/Passive
Self-blame/Blames-others
Logical/Emotional
Dedicated/Gives up
Flash Decisions/Contemplates
Wise/Foolish
Stubborn/Docile

Honest/Dishonest
Decisive/Indecisive
Forgiving/Grudges
Generous/Stingy
Warm/Cold
Grounded/Flighty
Reliable/Unreliable
Open/Secretive
Direct/Cautious/Daredevil
Dependent/Independent
Watcher/Participant
Night/Day
City/Country
Words/Fists
Neat/Messy
Focused/Distracted
Imaginative/Academic
Frugal/Wasteful
Flexible/Inflexible
Sweet/Sour/Bitter
Organized/Disorganized
Calm/Hot-tempered
Close/Long/Middle
Listens/Bullheaded
Generous/Selfish

Motivations: Wants or Needs: these often conflict.

_____
_____
_____
_____

What conflicts stand in the way?

_____
_____
_____

Notes:

_____
_____
_____
_____
_____

Story:	Role: MC, 2nd MC, 3rd MC, protagonist, antagonist, love interest, side kick, hapless bystander, other:
Book:	
Series:	Archetype: Tip: people have multiple facets. We don't pop out of molds.
Genre:	Primary Antagonist:

Name:
Tip: vary in first letter and length to limit confusion.

Age:

Eye Color:

Meaning:

DOB:

Hair Color:

Alias:

Height:

Hair Type:

Title:

Weight:

Hair Style:

Gender:

Build:

Skin Color:

Sexuality:

Blood Type:

Skin Tone:

Species:

Dominant Hand:

Voice:

Race:
Heritage born with.

Ethnicity:
Ethnicity is learned cultural behaviors.

Accent:
Tip: use with light touch.

Relationship Status:

Financial Status:

Social Class:

Identifying Features: injuries, scars, prosthetic, birthmarks, freckles, piercings, tattoos, alien features, biotech, scales, fangs, horns, ears, glasses, contacts, dimples, etc

Likes/Dislikes, Comforts/Fears, Strength/Weakness, Habits/Ticks

Character Traits

Tip: We are each a messy conflicted ball of contradictions. How can their own traits clash and force them to choose between two parts of themselves?

Introvert/Extrovert	Childish/Mature	Honest/Dishonest
Sarcastic/Quiet	Kind/Cruel/Uncaring	Decisive/Indecisive
Thinker/Feeler	Laidback/High-strung	Forgiving/Grudges
Judger/Perceiver	Cautious/Reckless	Generous/Stingy
Sensing/Intuition	Leader/Follower	Warm/Cold
Calm/Excitable	Loyal/Disloyal	Grounded/Flighty
Timid/Outgoing	Suspicious/Trusting	Reliable/Unreliable
Left Brain/Right Brain	Mouth-filter/No-mouth-filter	Open/Secretive
Pessimist/Optimist/Realist	Patient/Impatient	Direct/Cautious/Daredevil
Motivated/Unmotivated	Intelligent/Average/Dumb-as-a-rock	Dependent/Independent
Controlled/Impulsive		Watcher/Participant
Humble/Egotistical	Professional/Unprofessional	Night/Day
Polite/Rude	Formal/Informal	City/Country
A-B-O	Quiet/Loud	Words/Fists
Prioritizes/Procrastinates	Dominant/Submissive	Neat/Messy
Indoors/Outdoors	Early/Late/On-Time	Focused/Distracted
Efficient/Inefficient	Athletic/Sedentary	Imaginative/Academic
Agile/Clumsy/Strong	Frivolous/Conservative	Frugal/Wasteful
Fight/Flight	Routine/Spontaneity	Flexible/Inflexible
Mischievous/Serious	Competitive/Passive	Sweet/Sour/Bitter
Mature/Immature	Self-blame/Blames-others	Organized/Disorganized
Lazy/Hardworking	Logical/Emotional	Calm/Hot-tempered
Predator/Prey	Dedicated/Gives up	Close/Long/Middle
Common-Sense/Book-smarts	Flash Decisions/Contemplates	Listens/Bullheaded
	Wise/Foolish	Generous/Selfish
Private/TMI	Stubborn/Docile	

Motivations: Wants or Needs: these often conflict.

_____
_____
_____
_____

What conflicts stand in the way?

_____
_____
_____

Notes:

_____
_____
_____
_____
_____

Story:	Role: MC, 2nd MC, 3rd MC, protagonist, antagonist, love interest, side kick, hapless bystander, other:
Book:	
Series:	Archetype: Tip: people have multiple facets. We don't pop out of molds.
Genre:	Primary Antagonist:

Name:
Tip: vary in first letter and length to limit confusion.

Age:

Eye Color:

Meaning:

DOB:

Hair Color:

Alias:

Height:

Hair Type:

Title:

Weight:

Hair Style:

Gender:

Build:

Skin Color:

Sexuality:

Blood Type:

Skin Tone:

Species:

Dominant Hand:

Voice:

Race:

Heritage born with.

Ethnicity:

Ethnicity is learned cultural behaviors.

Accent:

Tip: use with light touch.

Relationship Status:

Financial Status:

Social Class:

Identifying Features: injuries, scars, prosthetic, birthmarks, freckles, piercings, tattoos, alien features, biotech, scales, fangs, horns, ears, glasses, contacts, dimples, etc

Likes/Dislikes, Comforts/Fears, Strength/Weakness, Habits/Ticks

Character Traits

Tip: We are each a messy conflicted ball of contradictions. How can their own traits clash and force them to choose between two parts of themselves?

Introvert/Extrovert
Sarcastic/Quiet
Thinker/Feeler
Judger/Perceiver
Sensing/Intuition
Calm/Excitable
Timid/Outgoing
Left Brain/Right Brain
Pessimist/Optimist/Realist
Motivated/Unmotivated
Controlled/Impulsive
Humble/Egotistical
Polite/Rude
A-B-O
Prioritizes/Procrastinates
Indoors/Outdoors
Efficient/Inefficient
Agile/Clumsy/Strong
Fight/Flight
Mischievous/Serious
Mature/Immature
Lazy/Hardworking
Predator/Prey
Common-Sense/Book-smarts
Private/TMI

Childish/Mature
Kind/Cruel/Uncaring
Laidback/High-strung
Cautious/Reckless
Leader/Follower
Loyal/Disloyal
Suspicious/Trusting
Mouth-filter/No-mouth-filter
Patient/Impatient
Intelligent/Average/Dumb-as-a-rock
Professional/Unprofessional
Formal/Informal
Quiet/Loud
Dominant/Submissive
Early/Late/On-Time
Athletic/Sedentary
Frivolous/Conservative
Routine/Spontaneity
Competitive/Passive
Self-blame/Blames-others
Logical/Emotional
Dedicated/Gives up
Flash Decisions/Contemplates
Wise/Foolish
Stubborn/Docile

Honest/Dishonest
Decisive/Indecisive
Forgiving/Grudges
Generous/Stingy
Warm/Cold
Grounded/Flighty
Reliable/Unreliable
Open/Secretive
Direct/Cautious/Daredevil
Dependent/Independent
Watcher/Participant
Night/Day
City/Country
Words/Fists
Neat/Messy
Focused/Distracted
Imaginative/Academic
Frugal/Wasteful
Flexible/Inflexible
Sweet/Sour/Bitter
Organized/Disorganized
Calm/Hot-tempered
Close/Long/Middle
Listens/Bullheaded
Generous/Selfish

Motivations: Wants or Needs: these often conflict.

_____
_____
_____
_____

What conflicts stand in the way?

_____
_____
_____

Notes:

_____
_____
_____
_____
_____

Story:	Role: MC, 2nd MC, 3rd MC, protagonist, antagonist, love interest, side kick, hapless bystander, other:
Book:	
Series:	Archetype: Tip: people have multiple facets. We don't pop out of molds.
Genre:	Primary Antagonist:

Name:
Tip: vary in first letter and length to limit confusion.

Age:

Eye Color:

Meaning:

DOB:

Hair Color:

Alias:

Height:

Hair Type:

Title:

Weight:

Hair Style:

Gender:

Build:

Skin Color:

Sexuality:

Blood Type:

Skin Tone:

Species:

Dominant Hand:

Voice:

Race:
Heritage born with.

Ethnicity:
Ethnicity is learned cultural behaviors.

Accent:
Tip: use with light touch.

Relationship Status:

Financial Status:

Social Class:

Identifying Features: injuries, scars, prosthetic, birthmarks, freckles, piercings, tattoos, alien features, biotech, scales, fangs, horns, ears, glasses, contacts, dimples, etc

Likes/Dislikes, Comforts/Fears, Strength/Weakness, Habits/Ticks

Character Traits

Tip: We are each a messy conflicted ball of contradictions. How can their own traits clash and force them to choose between two parts of themselves?

Introvert/Extrovert
Sarcastic/Quiet
Thinker/Feeler
Judger/Perceiver
Sensing/Intuition
Calm/Excitable
Timid/Outgoing
Left Brain/Right Brain
Pessimist/Optimist/Realist
Motivated/Unmotivated
Controlled/Impulsive
Humble/Egotistical
Polite/Rude
A-B-O
Prioritizes/Procrastinates
Indoors/Outdoors
Efficient/Inefficient
Agile/Clumsy/Strong
Fight/Flight
Mischievous/Serious
Mature/Immature
Lazy/Hardworking
Predator/Prey
Common-Sense/Book-smarts
Private/TMI

Childish/Mature
Kind/Cruel/Uncaring
Laidback/High-strung
Cautious/Reckless
Leader/Follower
Loyal/Disloyal
Suspicious/Trusting
Mouth-filter/No-mouth-filter
Patient/Impatient
Intelligent/Average/Dumb-as-a-rock
Professional/Unprofessional
Formal/Informal
Quiet/Loud
Dominant/Submissive
Early/Late/On-Time
Athletic/Sedentary
Frivolous/Conservative
Routine/Spontaneity
Competitive/Passive
Self-blame/Blames-others
Logical/Emotional
Dedicated/Gives up
Flash Decisions/Contemplates
Wise/Foolish
Stubborn/Docile

Honest/Dishonest
Decisive/Indecisive
Forgiving/Grudges
Generous/Stingy
Warm/Cold
Grounded/Flighty
Reliable/Unreliable
Open/Secretive
Direct/Cautious/Daredevil
Dependent/Independent
Watcher/Participant
Night/Day
City/Country
Words/Fists
Neat/Messy
Focused/Distracted
Imaginative/Academic
Frugal/Wasteful
Flexible/Inflexible
Sweet/Sour/Bitter
Organized/Disorganized
Calm/Hot-tempered
Close/Long/Middle
Listens/Bullheaded
Generous/Selfish

Motivations: Wants or Needs: these often conflict.

_____
_____
_____
_____

What conflicts stand in the way?

_____
_____
_____

Notes:

_____
_____
_____
_____
_____

Story:	Role: MC, 2nd MC, 3rd MC, protagonist, antagonist, love interest, side kick, hapless bystander, other:
Book:	
Series:	Archetype: Tip: people have multiple facets. We don't pop out of molds.
Genre:	Primary Antagonist:

Name:
Tip: vary in first letter and length to limit confusion.

Age:

Eye Color:

Meaning:

DOB:

Hair Color:

Alias:

Height:

Hair Type:

Title:

Weight:

Hair Style:

Gender:

Build:

Skin Color:

Sexuality:

Blood Type:

Skin Tone:

Species:

Dominant Hand:

Voice:

Race:

Heritage born with.

Ethnicity:
Ethnicity is learned cultural behaviors.

Accent:
Tip: use with light touch.

Relationship Status:

Financial Status:

Social Class:

Identifying Features: injuries, scars, prosthetic, birthmarks, freckles, piercings, tattoos, alien features, biotech, scales, fangs, horns, ears, glasses, contacts, dimples, etc

Likes/Dislikes, Comforts/Fears, Strength/Weakness, Habits/Ticks

Character Traits

Tip: We are each a messy conflicted ball of contradictions. How can their own traits clash and force them to choose between two parts of themselves?

Introvert/Extrovert
Sarcastic/Quiet
Thinker/Feeler
Judger/Perceiver
Sensing/Intuition
Calm/Excitable
Timid/Outgoing
Left Brain/Right Brain
Pessimist/Optimist/Realist
Motivated/Unmotivated
Controlled/Impulsive
Humble/Egotistical
Polite/Rude
A-B-O
Prioritizes/Procrastinates
Indoors/Outdoors
Efficient/Inefficient
Agile/Clumsy/Strong
Fight/Flight
Mischievous/Serious
Mature/Immature
Lazy/Hardworking
Predator/Prey
Common-Sense/Book-smarts
Private/TMI

Childish/Mature
Kind/Cruel/Uncaring
Laidback/High-strung
Cautious/Reckless
Leader/Follower
Loyal/Disloyal
Suspicious/Trusting
Mouth-filter/No-mouth-filter
Patient/Impatient
Intelligent/Average/Dumb-as-a-rock
Professional/Unprofessional
Formal/Informal
Quiet/Loud
Dominant/Submissive
Early/Late/On-Time
Athletic/Sedentary
Frivolous/Conservative
Routine/Spontaneity
Competitive/Passive
Self-blame/Blames-others
Logical/Emotional
Dedicated/Gives up
Flash Decisions/Contemplates
Wise/Foolish
Stubborn/Docile

Honest/Dishonest
Decisive/Indecisive
Forgiving/Grudges
Generous/Stingy
Warm/Cold
Grounded/Flighty
Reliable/Unreliable
Open/Secretive
Direct/Cautious/Daredevil
Dependent/Independent
Watcher/Participant
Night/Day
City/Country
Words/Fists
Neat/Messy
Focused/Distracted
Imaginative/Academic
Frugal/Wasteful
Flexible/Inflexible
Sweet/Sour/Bitter
Organized/Disorganized
Calm/Hot-tempered
Close/Long/Middle
Listens/Bullheaded
Generous/Selfish

Motivations: Wants or Needs: these often conflict.

_____
_____
_____
_____

What conflicts stand in the way?

_____
_____
_____

Notes:

_____
_____
_____
_____
_____

Story:	Role: MC, 2nd MC, 3rd MC, protagonist, antagonist, love interest, side kick, hapless bystander, other:
Book:	
Series:	Archetype: Tip: people have multiple facets. We don't pop out of molds.
Genre:	Primary Antagonist:

Name:
Tip: vary in first letter and length to limit confusion.

Age:

Eye Color:

Meaning:

DOB:

Hair Color:

Alias:

Height:

Hair Type:

Title:

Weight:

Hair Style:

Gender:

Build:

Skin Color:

Sexuality:

Blood Type:

Skin Tone:

Species:

Dominant Hand:

Voice:

Race:

Heritage born with.

Ethnicity:
Ethnicity is learned cultural behaviors.

Accent:
Tip: use with light touch.

Relationship Status:

Financial Status:

Social Class:

Identifying Features: injuries, scars, prosthetic, birthmarks, freckles, piercings, tattoos, alien features, biotech, scales, fangs, horns, ears, glasses, contacts, dimples, etc

Likes/Dislikes, Comforts/Fears, Strength/Weakness, Habits/Ticks

Character Traits

Tip: We are each a messy conflicted ball of contradictions. How can their own traits clash and force them to choose between two parts of themselves?

Introvert/Extrovert
Sarcastic/Quiet
Thinker/Feeler
Judger/Perceiver
Sensing/Intuition
Calm/Excitable
Timid/Outgoing
Left Brain/Right Brain
Pessimist/Optimist/Realist
Motivated/Unmotivated
Controlled/Impulsive
Humble/Egotistical
Polite/Rude
A-B-O
Prioritizes/Procrastinates
Indoors/Outdoors
Efficient/Inefficient
Agile/Clumsy/Strong
Fight/Flight
Mischievous/Serious
Mature/Immature
Lazy/Hardworking
Predator/Prey
Common-Sense/Book-smarts
Private/TMI

Childish/Mature
Kind/Cruel/Uncaring
Laidback/High-strung
Cautious/Reckless
Leader/Follower
Loyal/Disloyal
Suspicious/Trusting
Mouth-filter/No-mouth-filter
Patient/Impatient
Intelligent/Average/Dumb-as-a-rock
Professional/Unprofessional
Formal/Informal
Quiet/Loud
Dominant/Submissive
Early/Late/On-Time
Athletic/Sedentary
Frivolous/Conservative
Routine/Spontaneity
Competitive/Passive
Self-blame/Blames-others
Logical/Emotional
Dedicated/Gives up
Flash Decisions/Contemplates
Wise/Foolish
Stubborn/Docile

Honest/Dishonest
Decisive/Indecisive
Forgiving/Grudges
Generous/Stingy
Warm/Cold
Grounded/Flighty
Reliable/Unreliable
Open/Secretive
Direct/Cautious/Daredevil
Dependent/Independent
Watcher/Participant
Night/Day
City/Country
Words/Fists
Neat/Messy
Focused/Distracted
Imaginative/Academic
Frugal/Wasteful
Flexible/Inflexible
Sweet/Sour/Bitter
Organized/Disorganized
Calm/Hot-tempered
Close/Long/Middle
Listens/Bullheaded
Generous/Selfish

Motivations: Wants or Needs: these often conflict.

_____
_____
_____
_____

What conflicts stand in the way?

_____
_____
_____

Notes:

_____
_____
_____
_____
_____

Story:	Role: MC, 2nd MC, 3rd MC, protagonist, antagonist, love interest, side kick, hapless bystander, other:
Book:	
Series:	Archetype: Tip: people have multiple facets. We don't pop out of molds.
Genre:	Primary Antagonist:

Name:
Tip: vary in first letter and length to limit confusion.

Age:

Eye Color:

Meaning:

DOB:

Hair Color:

Alias:

Height:

Hair Type:

Title:

Weight:

Hair Style:

Gender:

Build:

Skin Color:

Sexuality:

Blood Type:

Skin Tone:

Species:

Dominant Hand:

Voice:

Race:
Heritage born with.

Ethnicity:
Ethnicity is learned cultural behaviors.

Accent:
Tip: use with light touch.

Relationship Status:

Financial Status:

Social Class:

Identifying Features: injuries, scars, prosthetic, birthmarks, freckles, piercings, tattoos, alien features, biotech, scales, fangs, horns, ears, glasses, contacts, dimples, etc

Likes/Dislikes, Comforts/Fears, Strength/Weakness, Habits/Ticks

Character Traits

Tip: We are each a messy conflicted ball of contradictions. How can their own traits clash and force them to choose between two parts of themselves?

Introvert/Extrovert
Sarcastic/Quiet
Thinker/Feeler
Judger/Perceiver
Sensing/Intuition
Calm/Excitable
Timid/Outgoing
Left Brain/Right Brain
Pessimist/Optimist/Realist
Motivated/Unmotivated
Controlled/Impulsive
Humble/Egotistical
Polite/Rude
A-B-O
Prioritizes/Procrastinates
Indoors/Outdoors
Efficient/Inefficient
Agile/Clumsy/Strong
Fight/Flight
Mischievous/Serious
Mature/Immature
Lazy/Hardworking
Predator/Prey
Common-Sense/Book-smarts
Private/TMI

Childish/Mature
Kind/Cruel/Uncaring
Laidback/High-strung
Cautious/Reckless
Leader/Follower
Loyal/Disloyal
Suspicious/Trusting
Mouth-filter/No-mouth-filter
Patient/Impatient
Intelligent/Average/Dumb-as-a-rock
Professional/Unprofessional
Formal/Informal
Quiet/Loud
Dominant/Submissive
Early/Late/On-Time
Athletic/Sedentary
Frivolous/Conservative
Routine/Spontaneity
Competitive/Passive
Self-blame/Blames-others
Logical/Emotional
Dedicated/Gives up
Flash Decisions/Contemplates
Wise/Foolish
Stubborn/Docile

Honest/Dishonest
Decisive/Indecisive
Forgiving/Grudges
Generous/Stingy
Warm/Cold
Grounded/Flighty
Reliable/Unreliable
Open/Secretive
Direct/Cautious/Daredevil
Dependent/Independent
Watcher/Participant
Night/Day
City/Country
Words/Fists
Neat/Messy
Focused/Distracted
Imaginative/Academic
Frugal/Wasteful
Flexible/Inflexible
Sweet/Sour/Bitter
Organized/Disorganized
Calm/Hot-tempered
Close/Long/Middle
Listens/Bullheaded
Generous/Selfish

Motivations: Wants or Needs: these often conflict.

_____
_____
_____
_____

What conflicts stand in the way?

_____
_____
_____

Notes:

_____
_____
_____
_____
_____

Story:	Role: MC, 2nd MC, 3rd MC, protagonist, antagonist, love interest, side kick, hapless bystander, other:
Book:	
Series:	Archetype: Tip: people have multiple facets. We don't pop out of molds.
Genre:	Primary Antagonist:

Name:
Tip: vary in first letter and length to limit confusion.

Age:

Eye Color:

Meaning:

DOB:

Hair Color:

Alias:

Height:

Hair Type:

Title:

Weight:

Hair Style:

Gender:

Build:

Skin Color:

Sexuality:

Blood Type:

Skin Tone:

Species:

Dominant Hand:

Voice:

Race:

Heritage born with.

Ethnicity:

Ethnicity is learned cultural behaviors.

Accent:

Tip: use with light touch.

Relationship Status:

Financial Status:

Social Class:

Identifying Features: injuries, scars, prosthetic, birthmarks, freckles, piercings, tattoos, alien features, biotech, scales, fangs, horns, ears, glasses, contacts, dimples, etc

Likes/Dislikes, Comforts/Fears, Strength/Weakness, Habits/Ticks

Character Traits

Tip: We are each a messy conflicted ball of contradictions. How can their own traits clash and force them to choose between two parts of themselves?

Introvert/Extrovert	Childish/Mature	Honest/Dishonest
Sarcastic/Quiet	Kind/Cruel/Uncaring	Decisive/Indecisive
Thinker/Feeler	Laidback/High-strung	Forgiving/Grudges
Judger/Perceiver	Cautious/Reckless	Generous/Stingy
Sensing/Intuition	Leader/Follower	Warm/Cold
Calm/Excitable	Loyal/Disloyal	Grounded/Flighty
Timid/Outgoing	Suspicious/Trusting	Reliable/Unreliable
Left Brain/Right Brain	Mouth-filter/No-mouth-filter	Open/Secretive
Pessimist/Optimist/Realist	Patient/Impatient	Direct/Cautious/Daredevil
Motivated/Unmotivated	Intelligent/Average/Dumb-as-a-rock	Dependent/Independent
Controlled/Impulsive	a-rock	Watcher/Participant
Humble/Egotistical	Professional/Unprofessional	Night/Day
Polite/Rude	Formal/Informal	City/Country
A-B-O	Quiet/Loud	Words/Fists
Prioritizes/Procrastinates	Dominant/Submissive	Neat/Messy
Indoors/Outdoors	Early/Late/On-Time	Focused/Distracted
Efficient/Inefficient	Athletic/Sedentary	Imaginative/Academic
Agile/Clumsy/Strong	Frivolous/Conservative	Frugal/Wasteful
Fight/Flight	Routine/Spontaneity	Flexible/Inflexible
Mischievous/Serious	Competitive/Passive	Sweet/Sour/Bitter
Mature/Immature	Self-blame/Blames-others	Organized/Disorganized
Lazy/Hardworking	Logical/Emotional	Calm/Hot-tempered
Predator/Prey	Dedicated/Gives up	Close/Long/Middle
Common-Sense/Book-smarts	Flash Decisions/Contemplates	Listens/Bullheaded
	Wise/Foolish	Generous/Selfish
Private/TMI	Stubborn/Docile	

Motivations: Wants or Needs: these often conflict.

_____
_____
_____
_____

What conflicts stand in the way?

_____
_____
_____

Notes:

_____
_____
_____
_____
_____

Story:	Role: MC, 2nd MC, 3rd MC, protagonist, antagonist, love interest, side kick, hapless bystander, other:
Book:	
Series:	Archetype: Tip: people have multiple facets. We don't pop out of molds.
Genre:	Primary Antagonist:

Name:
Tip: vary in first letter and length to limit confusion.

Age:

Eye Color:

Meaning:

DOB:

Hair Color:

Alias:

Height:

Hair Type:

Title:

Weight:

Hair Style:

Gender:

Build:

Skin Color:

Sexuality:

Blood Type:

Skin Tone:

Species:

Dominant Hand:

Voice:

Race:

Heritage born with.

Ethnicity:
Ethnicity is learned cultural behaviors.

Accent:
Tip: use with light touch.

Relationship Status:

Financial Status:

Social Class:

Identifying Features: injuries, scars, prosthetic, birthmarks, freckles, piercings, tattoos, alien features, biotech, scales, fangs, horns, ears, glasses, contacts, dimples, etc

Likes/Dislikes, Comforts/Fears, Strength/Weakness, Habits/Ticks

Character Traits

Tip: We are each a messy conflicted ball of contradictions. How can their own traits clash and force them to choose between two parts of themselves?

Introvert/Extrovert
Sarcastic/Quiet
Thinker/Feeler
Judger/Perceiver
Sensing/Intuition
Calm/Excitable
Timid/Outgoing
Left Brain/Right Brain
Pessimist/Optimist/Realist
Motivated/Unmotivated
Controlled/Impulsive
Humble/Egotistical
Polite/Rude
A-B-O
Prioritizes/Procrastinates
Indoors/Outdoors
Efficient/Inefficient
Agile/Clumsy/Strong
Fight/Flight
Mischievous/Serious
Mature/Immature
Lazy/Hardworking
Predator/Prey
Common-Sense/Book-smarts
Private/TMI

Childish/Mature
Kind/Cruel/Uncaring
Laidback/High-strung
Cautious/Reckless
Leader/Follower
Loyal/Disloyal
Suspicious/Trusting
Mouth-filter/No-mouth-filter
Patient/Impatient
Intelligent/Average/Dumb-as-a-rock
Professional/Unprofessional
Formal/Informal
Quiet/Loud
Dominant/Submissive
Early/Late/On-Time
Athletic/Sedentary
Frivolous/Conservative
Routine/Spontaneity
Competitive/Passive
Self-blame/Blames-others
Logical/Emotional
Dedicated/Gives up
Flash Decisions/Contemplates
Wise/Foolish
Stubborn/Docile

Honest/Dishonest
Decisive/Indecisive
Forgiving/Grudges
Generous/Stingy
Warm/Cold
Grounded/Flighty
Reliable/Unreliable
Open/Secretive
Direct/Cautious/Daredevil
Dependent/Independent
Watcher/Participant
Night/Day
City/Country
Words/Fists
Neat/Messy
Focused/Distracted
Imaginative/Academic
Frugal/Wasteful
Flexible/Inflexible
Sweet/Sour/Bitter
Organized/Disorganized
Calm/Hot-tempered
Close/Long/Middle
Listens/Bullheaded
Generous/Selfish

Motivations: Wants or Needs: these often conflict.

_____
_____
_____
_____

What conflicts stand in the way?

_____
_____
_____

Notes:

_____
_____
_____
_____
_____

Story:	Role: MC, 2nd MC, 3rd MC, protagonist, antagonist, love interest, side kick, hapless bystander, other:
Book:	
Series:	Archetype: Tip: people have multiple facets. We don't pop out of molds.
Genre:	Primary Antagonist:

Name:
Tip: vary in first letter and length to limit confusion.

Age:

Eye Color:

Meaning:

DOB:

Hair Color:

Alias:

Height:

Hair Type:

Title:

Weight:

Hair Style:

Gender:

Build:

Skin Color:

Sexuality:

Blood Type:

Skin Tone:

Species:

Dominant Hand:

Voice:

Race:
Heritage born with.

Ethnicity:
Ethnicity is learned cultural behaviors.

Accent:
Tip: use with light touch.

Relationship Status:

Financial Status:

Social Class:

Identifying Features: injuries, scars, prosthetic, birthmarks, freckles, piercings, tattoos, alien features, biotech, scales, fangs, horns, ears, glasses, contacts, dimples, etc

Likes/Dislikes, Comforts/Fears, Strength/Weakness, Habits/Ticks

Character Traits

Tip: We are each a messy conflicted ball of contradictions. How can their own traits clash and force them to choose between two parts of themselves?

Introvert/Extrovert
Sarcastic/Quiet
Thinker/Feeler
Judger/Perceiver
Sensing/Intuition
Calm/Excitable
Timid/Outgoing
Left Brain/Right Brain
Pessimist/Optimist/Realist
Motivated/Unmotivated
Controlled/Impulsive
Humble/Egotistical
Polite/Rude
A-B-O
Prioritizes/Procrastinates
Indoors/Outdoors
Efficient/Inefficient
Agile/Clumsy/Strong
Fight/Flight
Mischievous/Serious
Mature/Immature
Lazy/Hardworking
Predator/Prey
Common-Sense/Book-smarts
Private/TMI

Childish/Mature
Kind/Cruel/Uncaring
Laidback/High-strung
Cautious/Reckless
Leader/Follower
Loyal/Disloyal
Suspicious/Trusting
Mouth-filter/No-mouth-filter
Patient/Impatient
Intelligent/Average/Dumb-as-a-rock
Professional/Unprofessional
Formal/Informal
Quiet/Loud
Dominant/Submissive
Early/Late/On-Time
Athletic/Sedentary
Frivolous/Conservative
Routine/Spontaneity
Competitive/Passive
Self-blame/Blames-others
Logical/Emotional
Dedicated/Gives up
Flash Decisions/Contemplates
Wise/Foolish
Stubborn/Docile

Honest/Dishonest
Decisive/Indecisive
Forgiving/Grudges
Generous/Stingy
Warm/Cold
Grounded/Flighty
Reliable/Unreliable
Open/Secretive
Direct/Cautious/Daredevil
Dependent/Independent
Watcher/Participant
Night/Day
City/Country
Words/Fists
Neat/Messy
Focused/Distracted
Imaginative/Academic
Frugal/Wasteful
Flexible/Inflexible
Sweet/Sour/Bitter
Organized/Disorganized
Calm/Hot-tempered
Close/Long/Middle
Listens/Bullheaded
Generous/Selfish

Motivations: Wants or Needs: these often conflict.

_____
_____
_____
_____

What conflicts stand in the way?

_____
_____
_____

Notes:

_____
_____
_____
_____
_____

Story:	Role: MC, 2nd MC, 3rd MC, protagonist, antagonist, love interest, side kick, hapless bystander, other:
Book:	
Series:	Archetype: Tip: people have multiple facets. We don't pop out of molds.
Genre:	Primary Antagonist:

Name:
Tip: vary in first letter and length to limit confusion.

Age:

Eye Color:

Meaning:

DOB:

Hair Color:

Alias:

Height:

Hair Type:

Title:

Weight:

Hair Style:

Gender:

Build:

Skin Color:

Sexuality:

Blood Type:

Skin Tone:

Species:

Dominant Hand:

Voice:

Race:
Heritage born with.

Ethnicity:
Ethnicity is learned cultural behaviors.

Accent:
Tip: use with light touch.

Relationship Status:

Financial Status:

Social Class:

Identifying Features: injuries, scars, prosthetic, birthmarks, freckles, piercings, tattoos, alien features, biotech, scales, fangs, horns, ears, glasses, contacts, dimples, etc

Likes/Dislikes, Comforts/Fears, Strength/Weakness, Habits/Ticks

Character Traits

Tip: We are each a messy conflicted ball of contradictions. How can their own traits clash and force them to choose between two parts of themselves?

Introvert/Extrovert
Sarcastic/Quiet
Thinker/Feeler
Judger/Perceiver
Sensing/Intuition
Calm/Excitable
Timid/Outgoing
Left Brain/Right Brain
Pessimist/Optimist/Realist
Motivated/Unmotivated
Controlled/Impulsive
Humble/Egotistical
Polite/Rude
A-B-O
Prioritizes/Procrastinates
Indoors/Outdoors
Efficient/Inefficient
Agile/Clumsy/Strong
Fight/Flight
Mischievous/Serious
Mature/Immature
Lazy/Hardworking
Predator/Prey
Common-Sense/Book-smarts
Private/TMI

Childish/Mature
Kind/Cruel/Uncaring
Laidback/High-strung
Cautious/Reckless
Leader/Follower
Loyal/Disloyal
Suspicious/Trusting
Mouth-filter/No-mouth-filter
Patient/Impatient
Intelligent/Average/Dumb-as-a-rock
Professional/Unprofessional
Formal/Informal
Quiet/Loud
Dominant/Submissive
Early/Late/On-Time
Athletic/Sedentary
Frivolous/Conservative
Routine/Spontaneity
Competitive/Passive
Self-blame/Blames-others
Logical/Emotional
Dedicated/Gives up
Flash Decisions/Contemplates
Wise/Foolish
Stubborn/Docile

Honest/Dishonest
Decisive/Indecisive
Forgiving/Grudges
Generous/Stingy
Warm/Cold
Grounded/Flighty
Reliable/Unreliable
Open/Secretive
Direct/Cautious/Daredevil
Dependent/Independent
Watcher/Participant
Night/Day
City/Country
Words/Fists
Neat/Messy
Focused/Distracted
Imaginative/Academic
Frugal/Wasteful
Flexible/Inflexible
Sweet/Sour/Bitter
Organized/Disorganized
Calm/Hot-tempered
Close/Long/Middle
Listens/Bullheaded
Generous/Selfish

Motivations: Wants or Needs: these often conflict.

_____
_____
_____
_____

What conflicts stand in the way?

_____
_____
_____

Notes:

_____
_____
_____
_____
_____

Story:	Role: MC, 2nd MC, 3rd MC, protagonist, antagonist, love interest, side kick, hapless bystander, other:
Book:	
Series:	Archetype: Tip: people have multiple facets. We don't pop out of molds.
Genre:	Primary Antagonist:

Name:
Tip: vary in first letter and length to limit confusion.

Age:

Eye Color:

Meaning:

DOB:

Hair Color:

Alias:

Height:

Hair Type:

Title:

Weight:

Hair Style:

Gender:

Build:

Skin Color:

Sexuality:

Blood Type:

Skin Tone:

Species:

Dominant Hand:

Voice:

Race:

Heritage born with.

Ethnicity:

Ethnicity is learned cultural behaviors.

Accent:

Tip: use with light touch.

Relationship Status:

Financial Status:

Social Class:

Identifying Features: injuries, scars, prosthetic, birthmarks, freckles, piercings, tattoos, alien features, biotech, scales, fangs, horns, ears, glasses, contacts, dimples, etc

Likes/Dislikes, Comforts/Fears, Strength/Weakness, Habits/Ticks

Character Traits

Tip: We are each a messy conflicted ball of contradictions. How can their own traits clash and force them to choose between two parts of themselves?

Introvert/Extrovert
Sarcastic/Quiet
Thinker/Feeler
Judger/Perceiver
Sensing/Intuition
Calm/Excitable
Timid/Outgoing
Left Brain/Right Brain
Pessimist/Optimist/Realist
Motivated/Unmotivated
Controlled/Impulsive
Humble/Egotistical
Polite/Rude
A-B-O
Prioritizes/Procrastinates
Indoors/Outdoors
Efficient/Inefficient
Agile/Clumsy/Strong
Fight/Flight
Mischievous/Serious
Mature/Immature
Lazy/Hardworking
Predator/Prey
Common-Sense/Book-smarts
Private/TMI

Childish/Mature
Kind/Cruel/Uncaring
Laidback/High-strung
Cautious/Reckless
Leader/Follower
Loyal/Disloyal
Suspicious/Trusting
Mouth-filter/No-mouth-filter
Patient/Impatient
Intelligent/Average/Dumb-as-a-rock
Professional/Unprofessional
Formal/Informal
Quiet/Loud
Dominant/Submissive
Early/Late/On-Time
Athletic/Sedentary
Frivolous/Conservative
Routine/Spontaneity
Competitive/Passive
Self-blame/Blames-others
Logical/Emotional
Dedicated/Gives up
Flash Decisions/Contemplates
Wise/Foolish
Stubborn/Docile

Honest/Dishonest
Decisive/Indecisive
Forgiving/Grudges
Generous/Stingy
Warm/Cold
Grounded/Flighty
Reliable/Unreliable
Open/Secretive
Direct/Cautious/Daredevil
Dependent/Independent
Watcher/Participant
Night/Day
City/Country
Words/Fists
Neat/Messy
Focused/Distracted
Imaginative/Academic
Frugal/Wasteful
Flexible/Inflexible
Sweet/Sour/Bitter
Organized/Disorganized
Calm/Hot-tempered
Close/Long/Middle
Listens/Bullheaded
Generous/Selfish

Motivations: Wants or Needs: these often conflict.

_____
_____
_____
_____

What conflicts stand in the way?

_____
_____
_____

Notes:

_____
_____
_____
_____
_____

Story:	Role: MC, 2nd MC, 3rd MC, protagonist, antagonist, love interest, side kick, hapless bystander, other:
Book:	
Series:	Archetype: Tip: people have multiple facets. We don't pop out of molds.
Genre:	Primary Antagonist:

Name:
Tip: vary in first letter and length to limit confusion.

	Age:	Eye Color:
Meaning:	DOB:	Hair Color:
Alias:	Height:	Hair Type:
Title:	Weight:	Hair Style:
Gender:	Build:	Skin Color:
Sexuality:	Blood Type:	Skin Tone:
Species:	Dominant Hand:	Voice:

Race:

Heritage born with.

Ethnicity:

Ethnicity is learned cultural behaviors.

Accent:

Tip: use with light touch.

Relationship Status: Financial Status: Social Class:

Identifying Features: injuries, scars, prosthetic, birthmarks, freckles, piercings, tattoos, alien features, biotech, scales, fangs, horns, ears, glasses, contacts, dimples, etc

Likes/Dislikes, Comforts/Fears, Strength/Weakness, Habits/Ticks

Character Traits

Tip: We are each a messy conflicted ball of contradictions. How can their own traits clash and force them to choose between two parts of themselves?

Introvert/Extrovert	Childish/Mature	Honest/Dishonest
Sarcastic/Quiet	Kind/Cruel/Uncaring	Decisive/Indecisive
Thinker/Feeler	Laidback/High-strung	Forgiving/Grudges
Judger/Perceiver	Cautious/Reckless	Generous/Stingy
Sensing/Intuition	Leader/Follower	Warm/Cold
Calm/Excitable	Loyal/Disloyal	Grounded/Flighty
Timid/Outgoing	Suspicious/Trusting	Reliable/Unreliable
Left Brain/Right Brain	Mouth-filter/No-mouth-filter	Open/Secretive
Pessimist/Optimist/Realist	Patient/Impatient	Direct/Cautious/Daredevil
Motivated/Unmotivated	Intelligent/Average/Dumb-as-a-rock	Dependent/Independent
Controlled/Impulsive	Professional/Unprofessional	Watcher/Participant
Humble/Egotistical	Formal/Informal	Night/Day
Polite/Rude	Quiet/Loud	City/Country
A-B-O	Dominant/Submissive	Words/Fists
Prioritizes/Procrastinates	Early/Late/On-Time	Neat/Messy
Indoors/Outdoors	Athletic/Sedentary	Focused/Distracted
Efficient/Inefficient	Frivolous/Conservative	Imaginative/Academic
Agile/Clumsy/Strong	Routine/Spontaneity	Frugal/Wasteful
Fight/Flight	Competitive/Passive	Flexible/Inflexible
Mischievous/Serious	Self-blame/Blames-others	Sweet/Sour/Bitter
Mature/Immature	Logical/Emotional	Organized/Disorganized
Lazy/Hardworking	Dedicated/Gives up	Calm/Hot-tempered
Predator/Prey	Flash Decisions/Contemplates	Close/Long/Middle
Common-Sense/Book-smarts	Wise/Foolish	Listens/Bullheaded
Private/TMI	Stubborn/Docile	Generous/Selfish

Motivations: Wants or Needs: these often conflict.

_____
_____
_____
_____

What conflicts stand in the way?

_____
_____
_____

Notes:

_____
_____
_____
_____
_____

Story:	Role: MC, 2nd MC, 3rd MC, protagonist, antagonist, love interest, side kick, hapless bystander, other:
Book:	
Series:	Archetype: Tip: people have multiple facets. We don't pop out of molds.
Genre:	Primary Antagonist:

Name:
Tip: vary in first letter and length to limit confusion.

Age:

Eye Color:

Meaning:

DOB:

Hair Color:

Alias:

Height:

Hair Type:

Title:

Weight:

Hair Style:

Gender:

Build:

Skin Color:

Sexuality:

Blood Type:

Skin Tone:

Species:

Dominant Hand:

Voice:

Race:
Heritage born with.

Ethnicity:
Ethnicity is learned cultural behaviors.

Accent:
Tip: use with light touch.

Relationship Status:

Financial Status:

Social Class:

Identifying Features: injuries, scars, prosthetic, birthmarks, freckles, piercings, tattoos, alien features, biotech, scales, fangs, horns, ears, glasses, contacts, dimples, etc

Likes/Dislikes, Comforts/Fears, Strength/Weakness, Habits/Ticks

Character Traits

Tip: We are each a messy conflicted ball of contradictions. How can their own traits clash and force them to choose between two parts of themselves?

Introvert/Extrovert	Childish/Mature	Honest/Dishonest
Sarcastic/Quiet	Kind/Cruel/Uncaring	Decisive/Indecisive
Thinker/Feeler	Laidback/High-strung	Forgiving/Grudges
Judger/Perceiver	Cautious/Reckless	Generous/Stingy
Sensing/Intuition	Leader/Follower	Warm/Cold
Calm/Excitable	Loyal/Disloyal	Grounded/Flighty
Timid/Outgoing	Suspicious/Trusting	Reliable/Unreliable
Left Brain/Right Brain	Mouth-filter/No-mouth-filter	Open/Secretive
Pessimist/Optimist/Realist	Patient/Impatient	Direct/Cautious/Daredevil
Motivated/Unmotivated	Intelligent/Average/Dumb-as-a-rock	Dependent/Independent
Controlled/Impulsive		Watcher/Participant
Humble/Egotistical	Professional/Unprofessional	Night/Day
Polite/Rude	Formal/Informal	City/Country
A-B-O	Quiet/Loud	Words/Fists
Prioritizes/Procrastinates	Dominant/Submissive	Neat/Messy
Indoors/Outdoors	Early/Late/On-Time	Focused/Distracted
Efficient/Inefficient	Athletic/Sedentary	Imaginative/Academic
Agile/Clumsy/Strong	Frivolous/Conservative	Frugal/Wasteful
Fight/Flight	Routine/Spontaneity	Flexible/Inflexible
Mischievous/Serious	Competitive/Passive	Sweet/Sour/Bitter
Mature/Immature	Self-blame/Blames-others	Organized/Disorganized
Lazy/Hardworking	Logical/Emotional	Calm/Hot-tempered
Predator/Prey	Dedicated/Gives up	Close/Long/Middle
Common-Sense/Book-smarts	Flash Decisions/Contemplates	Listens/Bullheaded
	Wise/Foolish	Generous/Selfish
Private/TMI	Stubborn/Docile	

Motivations: Wants or Needs: these often conflict.

_____
_____
_____
_____

What conflicts stand in the way?

_____
_____
_____

Notes:

_____
_____
_____
_____
_____

Story:	Role: MC, 2nd MC, 3rd MC, protagonist, antagonist, love interest, side kick, hapless bystander, other:
Book:	
Series:	Archetype: Tip: people have multiple facets. We don't pop out of molds.
Genre:	Primary Antagonist:

Name:
Tip: vary in first letter and length
to limit confusion.

Age:

Eye Color:

Meaning:

DOB:

Hair Color:

Alias:

Height:

Hair Type:

Title:

Weight:

Hair Style:

Gender:

Build:

Skin Color:

Sexuality:

Blood Type:

Skin Tone:

Species:

Dominant Hand:

Voice:

Race:

Heritage born with.

Ethnicity:

Ethnicity is learned cultural
behaviors.

Accent:

Tip: use with light touch.

Relationship Status:

Financial Status:

Social Class:

Identifying Features: injuries, scars, prosthetic, birthmarks, freckles, piercings, tattoos, alien
features, biotech, scales, fangs, horns, ears, glasses, contacts, dimples, etc

Likes/Dislikes, Comforts/Fears, Strength/Weakness, Habits/Ticks

Character Traits

Tip: We are each a messy conflicted ball of contradictions. How can their own traits clash and force them to choose between two parts of themselves?

Introvert/Extrovert
Sarcastic/Quiet
Thinker/Feeler
Judger/Perceiver
Sensing/Intuition
Calm/Excitable
Timid/Outgoing
Left Brain/Right Brain
Pessimist/Optimist/Realist
Motivated/Unmotivated
Controlled/Impulsive
Humble/Egotistical
Polite/Rude
A-B-O
Prioritizes/Procrastinates
Indoors/Outdoors
Efficient/Inefficient
Agile/Clumsy/Strong
Fight/Flight
Mischievous/Serious
Mature/Immature
Lazy/Hardworking
Predator/Prey
Common-Sense/Book-smarts
Private/TMI

Childish/Mature
Kind/Cruel/Uncaring
Laidback/High-strung
Cautious/Reckless
Leader/Follower
Loyal/Disloyal
Suspicious/Trusting
Mouth-filter/No-mouth-filter
Patient/Impatient
Intelligent/Average/Dumb-as-a-rock
Professional/Unprofessional
Formal/Informal
Quiet/Loud
Dominant/Submissive
Early/Late/On-Time
Athletic/Sedentary
Frivolous/Conservative
Routine/Spontaneity
Competitive/Passive
Self-blame/Blames-others
Logical/Emotional
Dedicated/Gives up
Flash Decisions/Contemplates
Wise/Foolish
Stubborn/Docile

Honest/Dishonest
Decisive/Indecisive
Forgiving/Grudges
Generous/Stingy
Warm/Cold
Grounded/Flighty
Reliable/Unreliable
Open/Secretive
Direct/Cautious/Daredevil
Dependent/Independent
Watcher/Participant
Night/Day
City/Country
Words/Fists
Neat/Messy
Focused/Distracted
Imaginative/Academic
Frugal/Wasteful
Flexible/Inflexible
Sweet/Sour/Bitter
Organized/Disorganized
Calm/Hot-tempered
Close/Long/Middle
Listens/Bullheaded
Generous/Selfish

Motivations: Wants or Needs: these often conflict.

_____
_____
_____
_____

What conflicts stand in the way?

_____
_____
_____

Notes:

_____
_____
_____
_____
_____

Story:	Role: MC, 2nd MC, 3rd MC, protagonist, antagonist, love interest, side kick, hapless bystander, other:
Book:	
Series:	Archetype: Tip: people have multiple facets. We don't pop out of molds.
Genre:	Primary Antagonist:

Name:
Tip: vary in first letter and length to limit confusion.

Age:

Eye Color:

Meaning:

DOB:

Hair Color:

Alias:

Height:

Hair Type:

Title:

Weight:

Hair Style:

Gender:

Build:

Skin Color:

Sexuality:

Blood Type:

Skin Tone:

Species:

Dominant Hand:

Voice:

Race:
Heritage born with.

Ethnicity:
Ethnicity is learned cultural behaviors.

Accent:
Tip: use with light touch.

Relationship Status:

Financial Status:

Social Class:

Identifying Features: injuries, scars, prosthetic, birthmarks, freckles, piercings, tattoos, alien features, biotech, scales, fangs, horns, ears, glasses, contacts, dimples, etc

Likes/Dislikes, Comforts/Fears, Strength/Weakness, Habits/Ticks

Character Traits

Tip: We are each a messy conflicted ball of contradictions. How can their own traits clash and force them to choose between two parts of themselves?

Introvert/Extrovert	Childish/Mature	Honest/Dishonest
Sarcastic/Quiet	Kind/Cruel/Uncaring	Decisive/Indecisive
Thinker/Feeler	Laidback/High-strung	Forgiving/Grudges
Judger/Perceiver	Cautious/Reckless	Generous/Stingy
Sensing/Intuition	Leader/Follower	Warm/Cold
Calm/Excitable	Loyal/Disloyal	Grounded/Flighty
Timid/Outgoing	Suspicious/Trusting	Reliable/Unreliable
Left Brain/Right Brain	Mouth-filter/No-mouth-filter	Open/Secretive
Pessimist/Optimist/Realist	Patient/Impatient	Direct/Cautious/Daredevil
Motivated/Unmotivated	Intelligent/Average/Dumb-as-	Dependent/Independent
Controlled/Impulsive	a-rock	Watcher/Participant
Humble/Egotistical	Professional/Unprofessional	Night/Day
Polite/Rude	Formal/Informal	City/Country
A-B-O	Quiet/Loud	Words/Fists
Prioritizes/Procrastinates	Dominant/Submissive	Neat/Messy
Indoors/Outdoors	Early/Late/On-Time	Focused/Distracted
Efficient/Inefficient	Athletic/Sedentary	Imaginative/Academic
Agile/Clumsy/Strong	Frivolous/Conservative	Frugal/Wasteful
Fight/Flight	Routine/Spontaneity	Flexible/Inflexible
Mischievous/Serious	Competitive/Passive	Sweet/Sour/Bitter
Mature/Immature	Self-blame/Blames-others	Organized/Disorganized
Lazy/Hardworking	Logical/Emotional	Calm/Hot-tempered
Predator/Prey	Dedicated/Gives up	Close/Long/Middle
Common-Sense/Book-	Flash Decisions/Contemplates	Listens/Bullheaded
smarts	Wise/Foolish	Generous/Selfish
Private/TMI	Stubborn/Docile	

Motivations: Wants or Needs: these often conflict.

_____
_____
_____
_____

What conflicts stand in the way?

_____
_____
_____

Notes:

_____
_____
_____
_____
_____

Story:	Role: MC, 2nd MC, 3rd MC, protagonist, antagonist, love interest, side kick, hapless bystander, other:
Book:	
Series:	Archetype: Tip: people have multiple facets. We don't pop out of molds.
Genre:	Primary Antagonist:

Name:
Tip: vary in first letter and length to limit confusion.

Age:

Eye Color:

Meaning:

DOB:

Hair Color:

Alias:

Height:

Hair Type:

Title:

Weight:

Hair Style:

Gender:

Build:

Skin Color:

Sexuality:

Blood Type:

Skin Tone:

Species:

Dominant Hand:

Voice:

Race:

Heritage born with.

Ethnicity:
Ethnicity is learned cultural behaviors.

Accent:
Tip: use with light touch.

Relationship Status:

Financial Status:

Social Class:

Identifying Features: injuries, scars, prosthetic, birthmarks, freckles, piercings, tattoos, alien features, biotech, scales, fangs, horns, ears, glasses, contacts, dimples, etc

Likes/Dislikes, Comforts/Fears, Strength/Weakness, Habits/Ticks

Character Traits

Tip: We are each a messy conflicted ball of contradictions. How can their own traits clash and force them to choose between two parts of themselves?

Introvert/Extrovert	Childish/Mature	Honest/Dishonest
Sarcastic/Quiet	Kind/Cruel/Uncaring	Decisive/Indecisive
Thinker/Feeler	Laidback/High-strung	Forgiving/Grudges
Judger/Perceiver	Cautious/Reckless	Generous/Stingy
Sensing/Intuition	Leader/Follower	Warm/Cold
Calm/Excitable	Loyal/Disloyal	Grounded/Flighty
Timid/Outgoing	Suspicious/Trusting	Reliable/Unreliable
Left Brain/Right Brain	Mouth-filter/No-mouth-filter	Open/Secretive
Pessimist/Optimist/Realist	Patient/Impatient	Direct/Cautious/Daredevil
Motivated/Unmotivated	Intelligent/Average/Dumb-as-a-rock	Dependent/Independent
Controlled/Impulsive		Watcher/Participant
Humble/Egotistical	Professional/Unprofessional	Night/Day
Polite/Rude	Formal/Informal	City/Country
A-B-O	Quiet/Loud	Words/Fists
Prioritizes/Procrastinates	Dominant/Submissive	Neat/Messy
Indoors/Outdoors	Early/Late/On-Time	Focused/Distracted
Efficient/Inefficient	Athletic/Sedentary	Imaginative/Academic
Agile/Clumsy/Strong	Frivolous/Conservative	Frugal/Wasteful
Fight/Flight	Routine/Spontaneity	Flexible/Inflexible
Mischievous/Serious	Competitive/Passive	Sweet/Sour/Bitter
Mature/Immature	Self-blame/Blames-others	Organized/Disorganized
Lazy/Hardworking	Logical/Emotional	Calm/Hot-tempered
Predator/Prey	Dedicated/Gives up	Close/Long/Middle
Common-Sense/Book-smarts	Flash Decisions/Contemplates	Listens/Bullheaded
	Wise/Foolish	Generous/Selfish
Private/TMI	Stubborn/Docile	

Motivations: Wants or Needs: these often conflict.

_____

_____

_____

_____

What conflicts stand in the way?

_____

_____

_____

Notes:

_____

_____

_____

_____

_____

Story:	Role: MC, 2nd MC, 3rd MC, protagonist, antagonist, love interest, side kick, hapless bystander, other:
Book:	
Series:	Archetype: Tip: people have multiple facets. We don't pop out of molds.
Genre:	Primary Antagonist:

Name:
Tip: vary in first letter and length to limit confusion.

Age:

Eye Color:

Meaning:

DOB:

Hair Color:

Alias:

Height:

Hair Type:

Title:

Weight:

Hair Style:

Gender:

Build:

Skin Color:

Sexuality:

Blood Type:

Skin Tone:

Species:

Dominant Hand:

Voice:

Race:
Heritage born with.

Ethnicity:
Ethnicity is learned cultural behaviors.

Accent:
Tip: use with light touch.

Relationship Status:

Financial Status:

Social Class:

Identifying Features: injuries, scars, prosthetic, birthmarks, freckles, piercings, tattoos, alien features, biotech, scales, fangs, horns, ears, glasses, contacts, dimples, etc

Likes/Dislikes, Comforts/Fears, Strength/Weakness, Habits/Ticks

Character Traits

Tip: We are each a messy conflicted ball of contradictions. How can their own traits clash and force them to choose between two parts of themselves?

Introvert/Extrovert
Sarcastic/Quiet
Thinker/Feeler
Judger/Perceiver
Sensing/Intuition
Calm/Excitable
Timid/Outgoing
Left Brain/Right Brain
Pessimist/Optimist/Realist
Motivated/Unmotivated
Controlled/Impulsive
Humble/Egotistical
Polite/Rude
A-B-O
Prioritizes/Procrastinates
Indoors/Outdoors
Efficient/Inefficient
Agile/Clumsy/Strong
Fight/Flight
Mischievous/Serious
Mature/Immature
Lazy/Hardworking
Predator/Prey
Common-Sense/Book-smarts
Private/TMI

Childish/Mature
Kind/Cruel/Uncaring
Laidback/High-strung
Cautious/Reckless
Leader/Follower
Loyal/Disloyal
Suspicious/Trusting
Mouth-filter/No-mouth-filter
Patient/Impatient
Intelligent/Average/Dumb-as-a-rock
Professional/Unprofessional
Formal/Informal
Quiet/Loud
Dominant/Submissive
Early/Late/On-Time
Athletic/Sedentary
Frivolous/Conservative
Routine/Spontaneity
Competitive/Passive
Self-blame/Blames-others
Logical/Emotional
Dedicated/Gives up
Flash Decisions/Contemplates
Wise/Foolish
Stubborn/Docile

Honest/Dishonest
Decisive/Indecisive
Forgiving/Grudges
Generous/Stingy
Warm/Cold
Grounded/Flighty
Reliable/Unreliable
Open/Secretive
Direct/Cautious/Daredevil
Dependent/Independent
Watcher/Participant
Night/Day
City/Country
Words/Fists
Neat/Messy
Focused/Distracted
Imaginative/Academic
Frugal/Wasteful
Flexible/Inflexible
Sweet/Sour/Bitter
Organized/Disorganized
Calm/Hot-tempered
Close/Long/Middle
Listens/Bullheaded
Generous/Selfish

Motivations: Wants or Needs: these often conflict.

_____
_____
_____
_____

What conflicts stand in the way?

_____
_____
_____

Notes:

_____
_____
_____
_____
_____

Story:	Role: MC, 2nd MC, 3rd MC, protagonist, antagonist, love interest, side kick, hapless bystander, other:
Book:	
Series:	Archetype: Tip: people have multiple facets. We don't pop out of molds.
Genre:	Primary Antagonist:

Name:
Tip: vary in first letter and length
to limit confusion.

Age:		Eye Color:

Meaning: DOB: Hair Color:

Alias: Height: Hair Type:

Title: Weight: Hair Style:

Gender: Build: Skin Color:

Sexuality: Blood Type: Skin Tone:

Species: Dominant Hand: Voice:

Race: **Ethnicity:**   **Accent:**
Heritage born with.   Ethnicity is learned cultural   Tip: use with light touch.
                  behaviors.

Relationship Status: Financial Status: Social Class:

Identifying Features: injuries, scars, prosthetic, birthmarks, freckles, piercings, tattoos, alien features, biotech, scales, fangs, horns, ears, glasses, contacts, dimples, etc

Likes/Dislikes, Comforts/Fears, Strength/Weakness, Habits/Ticks

Character Traits

Tip: We are each a messy conflicted ball of contradictions. How can their own traits clash and force them to choose between two parts of themselves?

Introvert/Extrovert
Sarcastic/Quiet
Thinker/Feeler
Judger/Perceiver
Sensing/Intuition
Calm/Excitable
Timid/Outgoing
Left Brain/Right Brain
Pessimist/Optimist/Realist
Motivated/Unmotivated
Controlled/Impulsive
Humble/Egotistical
Polite/Rude
A-B-O
Prioritizes/Procrastinates
Indoors/Outdoors
Efficient/Inefficient
Agile/Clumsy/Strong
Fight/Flight
Mischievous/Serious
Mature/Immature
Lazy/Hardworking
Predator/Prey
Common-Sense/Book-
smarts
Private/TMI

Childish/Mature
Kind/Cruel/Uncaring
Laidback/High-strung
Cautious/Reckless
Leader/Follower
Loyal/Disloyal
Suspicious/Trusting
Mouth-filter/No-mouth-filter
Patient/Impatient
Intelligent/Average/Dumb-as-
a-rock
Professional/Unprofessional
Formal/Informal
Quiet/Loud
Dominant/Submissive
Early/Late/On-Time
Athletic/Sedentary
Frivolous/Conservative
Routine/Spontaneity
Competitive/Passive
Self-blame/Blames-others
Logical/Emotional
Dedicated/Gives up
Flash Decisions/Contemplates
Wise/Foolish
Stubborn/Docile

Honest/Dishonest
Decisive/Indecisive
Forgiving/Grudges
Generous/Stingy
Warm/Cold
Grounded/Flighty
Reliable/Unreliable
Open/Secretive
Direct/Cautious/Daredevil
Dependent/Independent
Watcher/Participant
Night/Day
City/Country
Words/Fists
Neat/Messy
Focused/Distracted
Imaginative/Academic
Frugal/Wasteful
Flexible/Inflexible
Sweet/Sour/Bitter
Organized/Disorganized
Calm/Hot-tempered
Close/Long/Middle
Listens/Bullheaded
Generous/Selfish

Motivations: Wants or Needs: these often conflict.

_____
_____
_____
_____

What conflicts stand in the way?

_____
_____
_____

Notes:

_____
_____
_____
_____
_____

Story:	Role: MC, 2nd MC, 3rd MC, protagonist, antagonist, love interest, side kick, hapless bystander, other:
Book:	
Series:	Archetype: Tip: people have multiple facets. We don't pop out of molds.
Genre:	Primary Antagonist:

Name:
Tip: vary in first letter and length to limit confusion.

Age:

Eye Color:

Meaning:

DOB:

Hair Color:

Alias:

Height:

Hair Type:

Title:

Weight:

Hair Style:

Gender:

Build:

Skin Color:

Sexuality:

Blood Type:

Skin Tone:

Species:

Dominant Hand:

Voice:

Race:

Heritage born with.

Ethnicity:
Ethnicity is learned cultural behaviors.

Accent:
Tip: use with light touch.

Relationship Status:

Financial Status:

Social Class:

Identifying Features: injuries, scars, prosthetic, birthmarks, freckles, piercings, tattoos, alien features, biotech, scales, fangs, horns, ears, glasses, contacts, dimples, etc

Likes/Dislikes, Comforts/Fears, Strength/Weakness, Habits/Ticks

Character Traits

Tip: We are each a messy conflicted ball of contradictions. How can their own traits clash and force them to choose between two parts of themselves?

Introvert/Extrovert
Sarcastic/Quiet
Thinker/Feeler
Judger/Perceiver
Sensing/Intuition
Calm/Excitable
Timid/Outgoing
Left Brain/Right Brain
Pessimist/Optimist/Realist
Motivated/Unmotivated
Controlled/Impulsive
Humble/Egotistical
Polite/Rude
A-B-O
Prioritizes/Procrastinates
Indoors/Outdoors
Efficient/Inefficient
Agile/Clumsy/Strong
Fight/Flight
Mischievous/Serious
Mature/Immature
Lazy/Hardworking
Predator/Prey
Common-Sense/Book-smarts
Private/TMI

Childish/Mature
Kind/Cruel/Uncaring
Laidback/High-strung
Cautious/Reckless
Leader/Follower
Loyal/Disloyal
Suspicious/Trusting
Mouth-filter/No-mouth-filter
Patient/Impatient
Intelligent/Average/Dumb-as-a-rock
Professional/Unprofessional
Formal/Informal
Quiet/Loud
Dominant/Submissive
Early/Late/On-Time
Athletic/Sedentary
Frivolous/Conservative
Routine/Spontaneity
Competitive/Passive
Self-blame/Blames-others
Logical/Emotional
Dedicated/Gives up
Flash Decisions/Contemplates
Wise/Foolish
Stubborn/Docile

Honest/Dishonest
Decisive/Indecisive
Forgiving/Grudges
Generous/Stingy
Warm/Cold
Grounded/Flighty
Reliable/Unreliable
Open/Secretive
Direct/Cautious/Daredevil
Dependent/Independent
Watcher/Participant
Night/Day
City/Country
Words/Fists
Neat/Messy
Focused/Distracted
Imaginative/Academic
Frugal/Wasteful
Flexible/Inflexible
Sweet/Sour/Bitter
Organized/Disorganized
Calm/Hot-tempered
Close/Long/Middle
Listens/Bullheaded
Generous/Selfish

Motivations: Wants or Needs: these often conflict.

_____
_____
_____
_____

What conflicts stand in the way?

_____
_____
_____

Notes:

_____
_____
_____
_____
_____

Story:	Role: MC, 2nd MC, 3rd MC, protagonist, antagonist, love interest, side kick, hapless bystander, other:
Book:	
Series:	Archetype: Tip: people have multiple facets. We don't pop out of molds.
Genre:	Primary Antagonist:

Name:
Tip: vary in first letter and length to limit confusion.

Age:

Eye Color:

Meaning:

DOB:

Hair Color:

Alias:

Height:

Hair Type:

Title:

Weight:

Hair Style:

Gender:

Build:

Skin Color:

Sexuality:

Blood Type:

Skin Tone:

Species:

Dominant Hand:

Voice:

Race:
Heritage born with.

Ethnicity:
Ethnicity is learned cultural behaviors.

Accent:
Tip: use with light touch.

Relationship Status:

Financial Status:

Social Class:

Identifying Features: injuries, scars, prosthetic, birthmarks, freckles, piercings, tattoos, alien features, biotech, scales, fangs, horns, ears, glasses, contacts, dimples, etc

Likes/Dislikes, Comforts/Fears, Strength/Weakness, Habits/Ticks

Character Traits

Tip: We are each a messy conflicted ball of contradictions. How can their own traits clash and force them to choose between two parts of themselves?

Introvert/Extrovert
Sarcastic/Quiet
Thinker/Feeler
Judger/Perceiver
Sensing/Intuition
Calm/Excitable
Timid/Outgoing
Left Brain/Right Brain
Pessimist/Optimist/Realist
Motivated/Unmotivated
Controlled/Impulsive
Humble/Egotistical
Polite/Rude
A-B-O
Prioritizes/Procrastinates
Indoors/Outdoors
Efficient/Inefficient
Agile/Clumsy/Strong
Fight/Flight
Mischievous/Serious
Mature/Immature
Lazy/Hardworking
Predator/Prey
Common-Sense/Book-smarts
Private/TMI

Childish/Mature
Kind/Cruel/Uncaring
Laidback/High-strung
Cautious/Reckless
Leader/Follower
Loyal/Disloyal
Suspicious/Trusting
Mouth-filter/No-mouth-filter
Patient/Impatient
Intelligent/Average/Dumb-as-a-rock
Professional/Unprofessional
Formal/Informal
Quiet/Loud
Dominant/Submissive
Early/Late/On-Time
Athletic/Sedentary
Frivolous/Conservative
Routine/Spontaneity
Competitive/Passive
Self-blame/Blames-others
Logical/Emotional
Dedicated/Gives up
Flash Decisions/Contemplates
Wise/Foolish
Stubborn/Docile

Honest/Dishonest
Decisive/Indecisive
Forgiving/Grudges
Generous/Stingy
Warm/Cold
Grounded/Flighty
Reliable/Unreliable
Open/Secretive
Direct/Cautious/Daredevil
Dependent/Independent
Watcher/Participant
Night/Day
City/Country
Words/Fists
Neat/Messy
Focused/Distracted
Imaginative/Academic
Frugal/Wasteful
Flexible/Inflexible
Sweet/Sour/Bitter
Organized/Disorganized
Calm/Hot-tempered
Close/Long/Middle
Listens/Bullheaded
Generous/Selfish

Motivations: Wants or Needs: these often conflict.

_____
_____
_____
_____

What conflicts stand in the way?

_____
_____
_____

Notes:

_____
_____
_____
_____
_____

Story:	Role: MC, 2nd MC, 3rd MC, protagonist, antagonist, love interest, side kick, hapless bystander, other:
Book:	
Series:	Archetype: Tip: people have multiple facets. We don't pop out of molds.
Genre:	Primary Antagonist:

Name:
Tip: vary in first letter and length to limit confusion.

Age:

Eye Color:

Meaning:

DOB:

Hair Color:

Alias:

Height:

Hair Type:

Title:

Weight:

Hair Style:

Gender:

Build:

Skin Color:

Sexuality:

Blood Type:

Skin Tone:

Species:

Dominant Hand:

Voice:

Race:

Heritage born with.

Ethnicity:
Ethnicity is learned cultural behaviors.

Accent:
Tip: use with light touch.

Relationship Status:

Financial Status:

Social Class:

Identifying Features: injuries, scars, prosthetic, birthmarks, freckles, piercings, tattoos, alien features, biotech, scales, fangs, horns, ears, glasses, contacts, dimples, etc

Likes/Dislikes, Comforts/Fears, Strength/Weakness, Habits/Ticks

Character Traits

Tip: We are each a messy conflicted ball of contradictions. How can their own traits clash and force them to choose between two parts of themselves?

Introvert/Extrovert
Sarcastic/Quiet
Thinker/Feeler
Judger/Perceiver
Sensing/Intuition
Calm/Excitable
Timid/Outgoing
Left Brain/Right Brain
Pessimist/Optimist/Realist
Motivated/Unmotivated
Controlled/Impulsive
Humble/Egotistical
Polite/Rude
A-B-O
Prioritizes/Procrastinates
Indoors/Outdoors
Efficient/Inefficient
Agile/Clumsy/Strong
Fight/Flight
Mischievous/Serious
Mature/Immature
Lazy/Hardworking
Predator/Prey
Common-Sense/Book-smarts
Private/TMI

Childish/Mature
Kind/Cruel/Uncaring
Laidback/High-strung
Cautious/Reckless
Leader/Follower
Loyal/Disloyal
Suspicious/Trusting
Mouth-filter/No-mouth-filter
Patient/Impatient
Intelligent/Average/Dumb-as-a-rock
Professional/Unprofessional
Formal/Informal
Quiet/Loud
Dominant/Submissive
Early/Late/On-Time
Athletic/Sedentary
Frivolous/Conservative
Routine/Spontaneity
Competitive/Passive
Self-blame/Blames-others
Logical/Emotional
Dedicated/Gives up
Flash Decisions/Contemplates
Wise/Foolish
Stubborn/Docile

Honest/Dishonest
Decisive/Indecisive
Forgiving/Grudges
Generous/Stingy
Warm/Cold
Grounded/Flighty
Reliable/Unreliable
Open/Secretive
Direct/Cautious/Daredevil
Dependent/Independent
Watcher/Participant
Night/Day
City/Country
Words/Fists
Neat/Messy
Focused/Distracted
Imaginative/Academic
Frugal/Wasteful
Flexible/Inflexible
Sweet/Sour/Bitter
Organized/Disorganized
Calm/Hot-tempered
Close/Long/Middle
Listens/Bullheaded
Generous/Selfish

Motivations: Wants or Needs: these often conflict.

_____
_____
_____
_____

What conflicts stand in the way?

_____
_____
_____

Notes:

_____
_____
_____
_____
_____

Story:	Role: MC, 2nd MC, 3rd MC, protagonist, antagonist, love interest, side kick, hapless bystander, other:
Book:	
Series:	Archetype: Tip: people have multiple facets. We don't pop out of molds.
Genre:	Primary Antagonist:

Name:
Tip: vary in first letter and length to limit confusion.

Age:

Eye Color:

Meaning:

DOB:

Hair Color:

Alias:

Height:

Hair Type:

Title:

Weight:

Hair Style:

Gender:

Build:

Skin Color:

Sexuality:

Blood Type:

Skin Tone:

Species:

Dominant Hand:

Voice:

Race:
Heritage born with.

Ethnicity:
Ethnicity is learned cultural behaviors.

Accent:
Tip: use with light touch.

Relationship Status:

Financial Status:

Social Class:

Identifying Features: injuries, scars, prosthetic, birthmarks, freckles, piercings, tattoos, alien features, biotech, scales, fangs, horns, ears, glasses, contacts, dimples, etc

Likes/Dislikes, Comforts/Fears, Strength/Weakness, Habits/Ticks

Character Traits

Tip: We are each a messy conflicted ball of contradictions. How can their own traits clash and force them to choose between two parts of themselves?

Introvert/Extrovert
Sarcastic/Quiet
Thinker/Feeler
Judger/Perceiver
Sensing/Intuition
Calm/Excitable
Timid/Outgoing
Left Brain/Right Brain
Pessimist/Optimist/Realist
Motivated/Unmotivated
Controlled/Impulsive
Humble/Egotistical
Polite/Rude
A-B-O
Prioritizes/Procrastinates
Indoors/Outdoors
Efficient/Inefficient
Agile/Clumsy/Strong
Fight/Flight
Mischievous/Serious
Mature/Immature
Lazy/Hardworking
Predator/Prey
Common-Sense/Book-smarts
Private/TMI

Childish/Mature
Kind/Cruel/Uncaring
Laidback/High-strung
Cautious/Reckless
Leader/Follower
Loyal/Disloyal
Suspicious/Trusting
Mouth-filter/No-mouth-filter
Patient/Impatient
Intelligent/Average/Dumb-as-a-rock
Professional/Unprofessional
Formal/Informal
Quiet/Loud
Dominant/Submissive
Early/Late/On-Time
Athletic/Sedentary
Frivolous/Conservative
Routine/Spontaneity
Competitive/Passive
Self-blame/Blames-others
Logical/Emotional
Dedicated/Gives up
Flash Decisions/Contemplates
Wise/Foolish
Stubborn/Docile

Honest/Dishonest
Decisive/Indecisive
Forgiving/Grudges
Generous/Stingy
Warm/Cold
Grounded/Flighty
Reliable/Unreliable
Open/Secretive
Direct/Cautious/Daredevil
Dependent/Independent
Watcher/Participant
Night/Day
City/Country
Words/Fists
Neat/Messy
Focused/Distracted
Imaginative/Academic
Frugal/Wasteful
Flexible/Inflexible
Sweet/Sour/Bitter
Organized/Disorganized
Calm/Hot-tempered
Close/Long/Middle
Listens/Bullheaded
Generous/Selfish

Motivations: Wants or Needs: these often conflict.

_____
_____
_____
_____

What conflicts stand in the way?

_____
_____
_____

Notes:

_____
_____
_____
_____
_____

Story:	Role: MC, 2nd MC, 3rd MC, protagonist, antagonist, love interest, side kick, hapless bystander, other:
Book:	
Series:	Archetype: Tip: people have multiple facets. We don't pop out of molds.
Genre:	Primary Antagonist:

Name:
Tip: vary in first letter and length to limit confusion.

Age:

Eye Color:

Meaning:

DOB:

Hair Color:

Alias:

Height:

Hair Type:

Title:

Weight:

Hair Style:

Gender:

Build:

Skin Color:

Sexuality:

Blood Type:

Skin Tone:

Species:

Dominant Hand:

Voice:

Race:
Heritage born with.

Ethnicity:
Ethnicity is learned cultural behaviors.

Accent:
Tip: use with light touch.

Relationship Status:

Financial Status:

Social Class:

Identifying Features: injuries, scars, prosthetic, birthmarks, freckles, piercings, tattoos, alien features, biotech, scales, fangs, horns, ears, glasses, contacts, dimples, etc

Likes/Dislikes, Comforts/Fears, Strength/Weakness, Habits/Ticks

Character Traits

Tip: We are each a messy conflicted ball of contradictions. How can their own traits clash and force them to choose between two parts of themselves?

Introvert/Extrovert
Sarcastic/Quiet
Thinker/Feeler
Judger/Perceiver
Sensing/Intuition
Calm/Excitable
Timid/Outgoing
Left Brain/Right Brain
Pessimist/Optimist/Realist
Motivated/Unmotivated
Controlled/Impulsive
Humble/Egotistical
Polite/Rude
A-B-O
Prioritizes/Procrastinates
Indoors/Outdoors
Efficient/Inefficient
Agile/Clumsy/Strong
Fight/Flight
Mischievous/Serious
Mature/Immature
Lazy/Hardworking
Predator/Prey
Common-Sense/Book-smarts
Private/TMI

Childish/Mature
Kind/Cruel/Uncaring
Laidback/High-strung
Cautious/Reckless
Leader/Follower
Loyal/Disloyal
Suspicious/Trusting
Mouth-filter/No-mouth-filter
Patient/Impatient
Intelligent/Average/Dumb-as-a-rock
Professional/Unprofessional
Formal/Informal
Quiet/Loud
Dominant/Submissive
Early/Late/On-Time
Athletic/Sedentary
Frivolous/Conservative
Routine/Spontaneity
Competitive/Passive
Self-blame/Blames-others
Logical/Emotional
Dedicated/Gives up
Flash Decisions/Contemplates
Wise/Foolish
Stubborn/Docile

Honest/Dishonest
Decisive/Indecisive
Forgiving/Grudges
Generous/Stingy
Warm/Cold
Grounded/Flighty
Reliable/Unreliable
Open/Secretive
Direct/Cautious/Daredevil
Dependent/Independent
Watcher/Participant
Night/Day
City/Country
Words/Fists
Neat/Messy
Focused/Distracted
Imaginative/Academic
Frugal/Wasteful
Flexible/Inflexible
Sweet/Sour/Bitter
Organized/Disorganized
Calm/Hot-tempered
Close/Long/Middle
Listens/Bullheaded
Generous/Selfish

Motivations: Wants or Needs: these often conflict.

_____
_____
_____
_____

What conflicts stand in the way?

_____
_____
_____

Notes:

_____
_____
_____
_____
_____

Story:	Role: MC, 2nd MC, 3rd MC, protagonist, antagonist, love interest, side kick, hapless bystander, other:
Book:	
Series:	Archetype: Tip: people have multiple facets. We don't pop out of molds.
Genre:	Primary Antagonist:

Name:
Tip: vary in first letter and length to limit confusion.

Age:

Eye Color:

Meaning:

DOB:

Hair Color:

Alias:

Height:

Hair Type:

Title:

Weight:

Hair Style:

Gender:

Build:

Skin Color:

Sexuality:

Blood Type:

Skin Tone:

Species:

Dominant Hand:

Voice:

Race:
Heritage born with.

Ethnicity:
Ethnicity is learned cultural behaviors.

Accent:
Tip: use with light touch.

Relationship Status:

Financial Status:

Social Class:

Identifying Features: injuries, scars, prosthetic, birthmarks, freckles, piercings, tattoos, alien features, biotech, scales, fangs, horns, ears, glasses, contacts, dimples, etc

Likes/Dislikes, Comforts/Fears, Strength/Weakness, Habits/Ticks

Character Traits

Tip: We are each a messy conflicted ball of contradictions. How can their own traits clash and force them to choose between two parts of themselves?

Introvert/Extrovert
Sarcastic/Quiet
Thinker/Feeler
Judger/Perceiver
Sensing/Intuition
Calm/Excitable
Timid/Outgoing
Left Brain/Right Brain
Pessimist/Optimist/Realist
Motivated/Unmotivated
Controlled/Impulsive
Humble/Egotistical
Polite/Rude
A-B-O
Prioritizes/Procrastinates
Indoors/Outdoors
Efficient/Inefficient
Agile/Clumsy/Strong
Fight/Flight
Mischievous/Serious
Mature/Immature
Lazy/Hardworking
Predator/Prey
Common-Sense/Book-smarts
Private/TMI

Childish/Mature
Kind/Cruel/Uncaring
Laidback/High-strung
Cautious/Reckless
Leader/Follower
Loyal/Disloyal
Suspicious/Trusting
Mouth-filter/No-mouth-filter
Patient/Impatient
Intelligent/Average/Dumb-as-a-rock
Professional/Unprofessional
Formal/Informal
Quiet/Loud
Dominant/Submissive
Early/Late/On-Time
Athletic/Sedentary
Frivolous/Conservative
Routine/Spontaneity
Competitive/Passive
Self-blame/Blames-others
Logical/Emotional
Dedicated/Gives up
Flash Decisions/Contemplates
Wise/Foolish
Stubborn/Docile

Honest/Dishonest
Decisive/Indecisive
Forgiving/Grudges
Generous/Stingy
Warm/Cold
Grounded/Flighty
Reliable/Unreliable
Open/Secretive
Direct/Cautious/Daredevil
Dependent/Independent
Watcher/Participant
Night/Day
City/Country
Words/Fists
Neat/Messy
Focused/Distracted
Imaginative/Academic
Frugal/Wasteful
Flexible/Inflexible
Sweet/Sour/Bitter
Organized/Disorganized
Calm/Hot-tempered
Close/Long/Middle
Listens/Bullheaded
Generous/Selfish

Motivations: Wants or Needs: these often conflict.

_____
_____
_____
_____

What conflicts stand in the way?

_____
_____
_____

Notes:

_____
_____
_____
_____
_____

Story:	Role: MC, 2nd MC, 3rd MC, protagonist, antagonist, love interest, side kick, hapless bystander, other:
Book:	
Series:	Archetype: Tip: people have multiple facets. We don't pop out of molds.
Genre:	Primary Antagonist:

Name:
Tip: vary in first letter and length to limit confusion.

Age:

Eye Color:

Meaning:

DOB:

Hair Color:

Alias:

Height:

Hair Type:

Title:

Weight:

Hair Style:

Gender:

Build:

Skin Color:

Sexuality:

Blood Type:

Skin Tone:

Species:

Dominant Hand:

Voice:

Race:
Heritage born with.

Ethnicity:
Ethnicity is learned cultural behaviors.

Accent:
Tip: use with light touch.

Relationship Status:

Financial Status:

Social Class:

Identifying Features: injuries, scars, prosthetic, birthmarks, freckles, piercings, tattoos, alien features, biotech, scales, fangs, horns, ears, glasses, contacts, dimples, etc

Likes/Dislikes, Comforts/Fears, Strength/Weakness, Habits/Ticks

Character Traits

Tip: We are each a messy conflicted ball of contradictions. How can their own traits clash and force them to choose between two parts of themselves?

Introvert/Extrovert
Sarcastic/Quiet
Thinker/Feeler
Judger/Perceiver
Sensing/Intuition
Calm/Excitable
Timid/Outgoing
Left Brain/Right Brain
Pessimist/Optimist/Realist
Motivated/Unmotivated
Controlled/Impulsive
Humble/Egotistical
Polite/Rude
A-B-O
Prioritizes/Procrastinates
Indoors/Outdoors
Efficient/Inefficient
Agile/Clumsy/Strong
Fight/Flight
Mischievous/Serious
Mature/Immature
Lazy/Hardworking
Predator/Prey
Common-Sense/Book-smarts
Private/TMI

Childish/Mature
Kind/Cruel/Uncaring
Laidback/High-strung
Cautious/Reckless
Leader/Follower
Loyal/Disloyal
Suspicious/Trusting
Mouth-filter/No-mouth-filter
Patient/Impatient
Intelligent/Average/Dumb-as-a-rock
Professional/Unprofessional
Formal/Informal
Quiet/Loud
Dominant/Submissive
Early/Late/On-Time
Athletic/Sedentary
Frivolous/Conservative
Routine/Spontaneity
Competitive/Passive
Self-blame/Blames-others
Logical/Emotional
Dedicated/Gives up
Flash Decisions/Contemplates
Wise/Foolish
Stubborn/Docile

Honest/Dishonest
Decisive/Indecisive
Forgiving/Grudges
Generous/Stingy
Warm/Cold
Grounded/Flighty
Reliable/Unreliable
Open/Secretive
Direct/Cautious/Daredevil
Dependent/Independent
Watcher/Participant
Night/Day
City/Country
Words/Fists
Neat/Messy
Focused/Distracted
Imaginative/Academic
Frugal/Wasteful
Flexible/Inflexible
Sweet/Sour/Bitter
Organized/Disorganized
Calm/Hot-tempered
Close/Long/Middle
Listens/Bullheaded
Generous/Selfish

Motivations: Wants or Needs: these often conflict.

_____
_____
_____
_____

What conflicts stand in the way?

_____
_____
_____

Notes:

_____
_____
_____
_____
_____

Story:	Role: MC, 2nd MC, 3rd MC, protagonist, antagonist, love interest, side kick, hapless bystander, other:
Book:	
Series:	Archetype: Tip: people have multiple facets. We don't pop out of molds.
Genre:	Primary Antagonist:

Name:
Tip: vary in first letter and length to limit confusion.

Age:

Eye Color:

Meaning:

DOB:

Hair Color:

Alias:

Height:

Hair Type:

Title:

Weight:

Hair Style:

Gender:

Build:

Skin Color:

Sexuality:

Blood Type:

Skin Tone:

Species:

Dominant Hand:

Voice:

Race:

Heritage born with.

Ethnicity:

Ethnicity is learned cultural behaviors.

Accent:

Tip: use with light touch.

Relationship Status:

Financial Status:

Social Class:

Identifying Features: injuries, scars, prosthetic, birthmarks, freckles, piercings, tattoos, alien features, biotech, scales, fangs, horns, ears, glasses, contacts, dimples, etc

Likes/Dislikes, Comforts/Fears, Strength/Weakness, Habits/Ticks

Character Traits

Tip: We are each a messy conflicted ball of contradictions. How can their own traits clash and force them to choose between two parts of themselves?

Introvert/Extrovert
Sarcastic/Quiet
Thinker/Feeler
Judger/Perceiver
Sensing/Intuition
Calm/Excitable
Timid/Outgoing
Left Brain/Right Brain
Pessimist/Optimist/Realist
Motivated/Unmotivated
Controlled/Impulsive
Humble/Egotistical
Polite/Rude
A-B-O
Prioritizes/Procrastinates
Indoors/Outdoors
Efficient/Inefficient
Agile/Clumsy/Strong
Fight/Flight
Mischievous/Serious
Mature/Immature
Lazy/Hardworking
Predator/Prey
Common-Sense/Book-smarts
Private/TMI

Childish/Mature
Kind/Cruel/Uncaring
Laidback/High-strung
Cautious/Reckless
Leader/Follower
Loyal/Disloyal
Suspicious/Trusting
Mouth-filter/No-mouth-filter
Patient/Impatient
Intelligent/Average/Dumb-as-a-rock
Professional/Unprofessional
Formal/Informal
Quiet/Loud
Dominant/Submissive
Early/Late/On-Time
Athletic/Sedentary
Frivolous/Conservative
Routine/Spontaneity
Competitive/Passive
Self-blame/Blames-others
Logical/Emotional
Dedicated/Gives up
Flash Decisions/Contemplates
Wise/Foolish
Stubborn/Docile

Honest/Dishonest
Decisive/Indecisive
Forgiving/Grudges
Generous/Stingy
Warm/Cold
Grounded/Flighty
Reliable/Unreliable
Open/Secretive
Direct/Cautious/Daredevil
Dependent/Independent
Watcher/Participant
Night/Day
City/Country
Words/Fists
Neat/Messy
Focused/Distracted
Imaginative/Academic
Frugal/Wasteful
Flexible/Inflexible
Sweet/Sour/Bitter
Organized/Disorganized
Calm/Hot-tempered
Close/Long/Middle
Listens/Bullheaded
Generous/Selfish

Motivations: Wants or Needs: these often conflict.

_____
_____
_____
_____

What conflicts stand in the way?

_____
_____
_____

Notes:

_____
_____
_____
_____
_____

Story:	Role: MC, 2nd MC, 3rd MC, protagonist, antagonist, love interest, side kick, hapless bystander, other:
Book:	
Series:	Archetype: Tip: people have multiple facets. We don't pop out of molds.
Genre:	Primary Antagonist:

Name:
Tip: vary in first letter and length to limit confusion.

Age:

Eye Color:

Meaning:

DOB:

Hair Color:

Alias:

Height:

Hair Type:

Title:

Weight:

Hair Style:

Gender:

Build:

Skin Color:

Sexuality:

Blood Type:

Skin Tone:

Species:

Dominant Hand:

Voice:

Race:

Heritage born with.

Ethnicity:
Ethnicity is learned cultural behaviors.

Accent:
Tip: use with light touch.

Relationship Status:

Financial Status:

Social Class:

Identifying Features: injuries, scars, prosthetic, birthmarks, freckles, piercings, tattoos, alien features, biotech, scales, fangs, horns, ears, glasses, contacts, dimples, etc

Likes/Dislikes, Comforts/Fears, Strength/Weakness, Habits/Ticks

Character Traits

Tip: We are each a messy conflicted ball of contradictions. How can their own traits clash and force them to choose between two parts of themselves?

Introvert/Extrovert	Childish/Mature	Honest/Dishonest
Sarcastic/Quiet	Kind/Cruel/Uncaring	Decisive/Indecisive
Thinker/Feeler	Laidback/High-strung	Forgiving/Grudges
Judger/Perceiver	Cautious/Reckless	Generous/Stingy
Sensing/Intuition	Leader/Follower	Warm/Cold
Calm/Excitable	Loyal/Disloyal	Grounded/Flighty
Timid/Outgoing	Suspicious/Trusting	Reliable/Unreliable
Left Brain/Right Brain	Mouth-filter/No-mouth-filter	Open/Secretive
Pessimist/Optimist/Realist	Patient/Impatient	Direct/Cautious/Daredevil
Motivated/Unmotivated	Intelligent/Average/Dumb-as-	Dependent/Independent
Controlled/Impulsive	a-rock	Watcher/Participant
Humble/Egotistical	Professional/Unprofessional	Night/Day
Polite/Rude	Formal/Informal	City/Country
A-B-O	Quiet/Loud	Words/Fists
Prioritizes/Procrastinates	Dominant/Submissive	Neat/Messy
Indoors/Outdoors	Early/Late/On-Time	Focused/Distracted
Efficient/Inefficient	Athletic/Sedentary	Imaginative/Academic
Agile/Clumsy/Strong	Frivolous/Conservative	Frugal/Wasteful
Fight/Flight	Routine/Spontaneity	Flexible/Inflexible
Mischievous/Serious	Competitive/Passive	Sweet/Sour/Bitter
Mature/Immature	Self-blame/Blames-others	Organized/Disorganized
Lazy/Hardworking	Logical/Emotional	Calm/Hot-tempered
Predator/Prey	Dedicated/Gives up	Close/Long/Middle
Common-Sense/Book-	Flash Decisions/Contemplates	Listens/Bullheaded
smarts	Wise/Foolish	Generous/Selfish
Private/TMI	Stubborn/Docile	

Motivations: Wants or Needs: these often conflict.

_____

_____

_____

_____

What conflicts stand in the way?

_____

_____

_____

Notes:

_____

_____

_____

_____

_____

Story:	Role: MC, 2nd MC, 3rd MC, protagonist, antagonist, love interest, side kick, hapless bystander, other:
Book:	
Series:	Archetype: Tip: people have multiple facets. We don't pop out of molds.
Genre:	Primary Antagonist:

Name:
Tip: vary in first letter and length to limit confusion.

Age:

Eye Color:

Meaning:

DOB:

Hair Color:

Alias:

Height:

Hair Type:

Title:

Weight:

Hair Style:

Gender:

Build:

Skin Color:

Sexuality:

Blood Type:

Skin Tone:

Species:

Dominant Hand:

Voice:

Race:

Heritage born with.

Ethnicity:
Ethnicity is learned cultural behaviors.

Accent:
Tip: use with light touch.

Relationship Status:

Financial Status:

Social Class:

Identifying Features: injuries, scars, prosthetic, birthmarks, freckles, piercings, tattoos, alien features, biotech, scales, fangs, horns, ears, glasses, contacts, dimples, etc

Likes/Dislikes, Comforts/Fears, Strength/Weakness, Habits/Ticks

Character Traits

Tip: We are each a messy conflicted ball of contradictions. How can their own traits clash and force them to choose between two parts of themselves?

Introvert/Extrovert
Sarcastic/Quiet
Thinker/Feeler
Judger/Perceiver
Sensing/Intuition
Calm/Excitable
Timid/Outgoing
Left Brain/Right Brain
Pessimist/Optimist/Realist
Motivated/Unmotivated
Controlled/Impulsive
Humble/Egotistical
Polite/Rude
A-B-O
Prioritizes/Procrastinates
Indoors/Outdoors
Efficient/Inefficient
Agile/Clumsy/Strong
Fight/Flight
Mischievous/Serious
Mature/Immature
Lazy/Hardworking
Predator/Prey
Common-Sense/Book-smarts
Private/TMI

Childish/Mature
Kind/Cruel/Uncaring
Laidback/High-strung
Cautious/Reckless
Leader/Follower
Loyal/Disloyal
Suspicious/Trusting
Mouth-filter/No-mouth-filter
Patient/Impatient
Intelligent/Average/Dumb-as-a-rock
Professional/Unprofessional
Formal/Informal
Quiet/Loud
Dominant/Submissive
Early/Late/On-Time
Athletic/Sedentary
Frivolous/Conservative
Routine/Spontaneity
Competitive/Passive
Self-blame/Blames-others
Logical/Emotional
Dedicated/Gives up
Flash Decisions/Contemplates
Wise/Foolish
Stubborn/Docile

Honest/Dishonest
Decisive/Indecisive
Forgiving/Grudges
Generous/Stingy
Warm/Cold
Grounded/Flighty
Reliable/Unreliable
Open/Secretive
Direct/Cautious/Daredevil
Dependent/Independent
Watcher/Participant
Night/Day
City/Country
Words/Fists
Neat/Messy
Focused/Distracted
Imaginative/Academic
Frugal/Wasteful
Flexible/Inflexible
Sweet/Sour/Bitter
Organized/Disorganized
Calm/Hot-tempered
Close/Long/Middle
Listens/Bullheaded
Generous/Selfish

Motivations: Wants or Needs: these often conflict.

_____
_____
_____
_____

What conflicts stand in the way?

_____
_____
_____

Notes:

_____
_____
_____
_____
_____

Story:	Role: MC, 2nd MC, 3rd MC, protagonist, antagonist, love interest, side kick, hapless bystander, other:
Book:	
Series:	Archetype: Tip: people have multiple facets. We don't pop out of molds.
Genre:	Primary Antagonist:

Name:
Tip: vary in first letter and length to limit confusion.

Age:

Eye Color:

Meaning:

DOB:

Hair Color:

Alias:

Height:

Hair Type:

Title:

Weight:

Hair Style:

Gender:

Build:

Skin Color:

Sexuality:

Blood Type:

Skin Tone:

Species:

Dominant Hand:

Voice:

Race:
Heritage born with.

Ethnicity:
Ethnicity is learned cultural behaviors.

Accent:
Tip: use with light touch.

Relationship Status:

Financial Status:

Social Class:

Identifying Features: injuries, scars, prosthetic, birthmarks, freckles, piercings, tattoos, alien features, biotech, scales, fangs, horns, ears, glasses, contacts, dimples, etc

Likes/Dislikes, Comforts/Fears, Strength/Weakness, Habits/Ticks

Character Traits

Tip: We are each a messy conflicted ball of contradictions. How can their own traits clash and force them to choose between two parts of themselves?

Introvert/Extrovert
Sarcastic/Quiet
Thinker/Feeler
Judger/Perceiver
Sensing/Intuition
Calm/Excitable
Timid/Outgoing
Left Brain/Right Brain
Pessimist/Optimist/Realist
Motivated/Unmotivated
Controlled/Impulsive
Humble/Egotistical
Polite/Rude
A-B-O
Prioritizes/Procrastinates
Indoors/Outdoors
Efficient/Inefficient
Agile/Clumsy/Strong
Fight/Flight
Mischievous/Serious
Mature/Immature
Lazy/Hardworking
Predator/Prey
Common-Sense/Book-smarts
Private/TMI

Childish/Mature
Kind/Cruel/Uncaring
Laidback/High-strung
Cautious/Reckless
Leader/Follower
Loyal/Disloyal
Suspicious/Trusting
Mouth-filter/No-mouth-filter
Patient/Impatient
Intelligent/Average/Dumb-as-a-rock
Professional/Unprofessional
Formal/Informal
Quiet/Loud
Dominant/Submissive
Early/Late/On-Time
Athletic/Sedentary
Frivolous/Conservative
Routine/Spontaneity
Competitive/Passive
Self-blame/Blames-others
Logical/Emotional
Dedicated/Gives up
Flash Decisions/Contemplates
Wise/Foolish
Stubborn/Docile

Honest/Dishonest
Decisive/Indecisive
Forgiving/Grudges
Generous/Stingy
Warm/Cold
Grounded/Flighty
Reliable/Unreliable
Open/Secretive
Direct/Cautious/Daredevil
Dependent/Independent
Watcher/Participant
Night/Day
City/Country
Words/Fists
Neat/Messy
Focused/Distracted
Imaginative/Academic
Frugal/Wasteful
Flexible/Inflexible
Sweet/Sour/Bitter
Organized/Disorganized
Calm/Hot-tempered
Close/Long/Middle
Listens/Bullheaded
Generous/Selfish

Motivations: Wants or Needs: these often conflict.

_____
_____
_____
_____

What conflicts stand in the way?

_____
_____
_____

Notes:

_____
_____
_____
_____
_____

Story:	Role: MC, 2nd MC, 3rd MC, protagonist, antagonist, love interest, side kick, hapless bystander, other:
Book:	
Series:	Archetype: Tip: people have multiple facets. We don't pop out of molds.
Genre:	Primary Antagonist:

Name:
Tip: vary in first letter and length to limit confusion.

Age:

Eye Color:

Meaning:

DOB:

Hair Color:

Alias:

Height:

Hair Type:

Title:

Weight:

Hair Style:

Gender:

Build:

Skin Color:

Sexuality:

Blood Type:

Skin Tone:

Species:

Dominant Hand:

Voice:

Race:

Heritage born with.

Ethnicity:
Ethnicity is learned cultural behaviors.

Accent:
Tip: use with light touch.

Relationship Status:

Financial Status:

Social Class:

Identifying Features: injuries, scars, prosthetic, birthmarks, freckles, piercings, tattoos, alien features, biotech, scales, fangs, horns, ears, glasses, contacts, dimples, etc

Likes/Dislikes, Comforts/Fears, Strength/Weakness, Habits/Ticks

Character Traits

Tip: We are each a messy conflicted ball of contradictions. How can their own traits clash and force them to choose between two parts of themselves?

Introvert/Extrovert
Sarcastic/Quiet
Thinker/Feeler
Judger/Perceiver
Sensing/Intuition
Calm/Excitable
Timid/Outgoing
Left Brain/Right Brain
Pessimist/Optimist/Realist
Motivated/Unmotivated
Controlled/Impulsive
Humble/Egotistical
Polite/Rude
A-B-O
Prioritizes/Procrastinates
Indoors/Outdoors
Efficient/Inefficient
Agile/Clumsy/Strong
Fight/Flight
Mischievous/Serious
Mature/Immature
Lazy/Hardworking
Predator/Prey
Common-Sense/Book-smarts
Private/TMI

Childish/Mature
Kind/Cruel/Uncaring
Laidback/High-strung
Cautious/Reckless
Leader/Follower
Loyal/Disloyal
Suspicious/Trusting
Mouth-filter/No-mouth-filter
Patient/Impatient
Intelligent/Average/Dumb-as-a-rock
Professional/Unprofessional
Formal/Informal
Quiet/Loud
Dominant/Submissive
Early/Late/On-Time
Athletic/Sedentary
Frivolous/Conservative
Routine/Spontaneity
Competitive/Passive
Self-blame/Blames-others
Logical/Emotional
Dedicated/Gives up
Flash Decisions/Contemplates
Wise/Foolish
Stubborn/Docile

Honest/Dishonest
Decisive/Indecisive
Forgiving/Grudges
Generous/Stingy
Warm/Cold
Grounded/Flighty
Reliable/Unreliable
Open/Secretive
Direct/Cautious/Daredevil
Dependent/Independent
Watcher/Participant
Night/Day
City/Country
Words/Fists
Neat/Messy
Focused/Distracted
Imaginative/Academic
Frugal/Wasteful
Flexible/Inflexible
Sweet/Sour/Bitter
Organized/Disorganized
Calm/Hot-tempered
Close/Long/Middle
Listens/Bullheaded
Generous/Selfish

Motivations: Wants or Needs: these often conflict.

_____
_____
_____
_____

What conflicts stand in the way?

_____
_____
_____

Notes:

_____
_____
_____
_____
_____

Story:	Role: MC, 2nd MC, 3rd MC, protagonist, antagonist, love interest, side kick, hapless bystander, other:
Book:	
Series:	Archetype: Tip: people have multiple facets. We don't pop out of molds.
Genre:	Primary Antagonist:

Name:
Tip: vary in first letter and length to limit confusion.

Age:

Eye Color:

Meaning:

DOB:

Hair Color:

Alias:

Height:

Hair Type:

Title:

Weight:

Hair Style:

Gender:

Build:

Skin Color:

Sexuality:

Blood Type:

Skin Tone:

Species:

Dominant Hand:

Voice:

Race:

Heritage born with.

Ethnicity:

Ethnicity is learned cultural behaviors.

Accent:

Tip: use with light touch.

Relationship Status:

Financial Status:

Social Class:

Identifying Features: injuries, scars, prosthetic, birthmarks, freckles, piercings, tattoos, alien features, biotech, scales, fangs, horns, ears, glasses, contacts, dimples, etc

Likes/Dislikes, Comforts/Fears, Strength/Weakness, Habits/Ticks

Character Traits

Tip: We are each a messy conflicted ball of contradictions. How can their own traits clash and force them to choose between two parts of themselves?

Introvert/Extrovert
Sarcastic/Quiet
Thinker/Feeler
Judger/Perceiver
Sensing/Intuition
Calm/Excitable
Timid/Outgoing
Left Brain/Right Brain
Pessimist/Optimist/Realist
Motivated/Unmotivated
Controlled/Impulsive
Humble/Egotistical
Polite/Rude
A-B-O
Prioritizes/Procrastinates
Indoors/Outdoors
Efficient/Inefficient
Agile/Clumsy/Strong
Fight/Flight
Mischievous/Serious
Mature/Immature
Lazy/Hardworking
Predator/Prey
Common-Sense/Book-smarts
Private/TMI

Childish/Mature
Kind/Cruel/Uncaring
Laidback/High-strung
Cautious/Reckless
Leader/Follower
Loyal/Disloyal
Suspicious/Trusting
Mouth-filter/No-mouth-filter
Patient/Impatient
Intelligent/Average/Dumb-as-a-rock
Professional/Unprofessional
Formal/Informal
Quiet/Loud
Dominant/Submissive
Early/Late/On-Time
Athletic/Sedentary
Frivolous/Conservative
Routine/Spontaneity
Competitive/Passive
Self-blame/Blames-others
Logical/Emotional
Dedicated/Gives up
Flash Decisions/Contemplates
Wise/Foolish
Stubborn/Docile

Honest/Dishonest
Decisive/Indecisive
Forgiving/Grudges
Generous/Stingy
Warm/Cold
Grounded/Flighty
Reliable/Unreliable
Open/Secretive
Direct/Cautious/Daredevil
Dependent/Independent
Watcher/Participant
Night/Day
City/Country
Words/Fists
Neat/Messy
Focused/Distracted
Imaginative/Academic
Frugal/Wasteful
Flexible/Inflexible
Sweet/Sour/Bitter
Organized/Disorganized
Calm/Hot-tempered
Close/Long/Middle
Listens/Bullheaded
Generous/Selfish

Motivations: Wants or Needs: these often conflict.

_____
_____
_____
_____

What conflicts stand in the way?

_____
_____
_____

Notes:

_____
_____
_____
_____
_____

Story:	Role: MC, 2nd MC, 3rd MC, protagonist, antagonist, love interest, side kick, hapless bystander, other:
Book:	
Series:	Archetype: Tip: people have multiple facets. We don't pop out of molds.
Genre:	Primary Antagonist:

Name:
Tip: vary in first letter and length to limit confusion.

Meaning:

Alias:

Title:

Gender:

Sexuality:

Species:

Age:

DOB:

Height:

Weight:

Build:

Blood Type:

Dominant Hand:

Eye Color:

Hair Color:

Hair Type:

Hair Style:

Skin Color:

Skin Tone:

Voice:

Race:

Heritage born with.

Ethnicity:
Ethnicity is learned cultural behaviors.

Accent:
Tip: use with light touch.

Relationship Status:

Financial Status:

Social Class:

Identifying Features: injuries, scars, prosthetic, birthmarks, freckles, piercings, tattoos, alien features, biotech, scales, fangs, horns, ears, glasses, contacts, dimples, etc

Likes/Dislikes, Comforts/Fears, Strength/Weakness, Habits/Ticks

Character Traits

Tip: We are each a messy conflicted ball of contradictions. How can their own traits clash and force them to choose between two parts of themselves?

Introvert/Extrovert
Sarcastic/Quiet
Thinker/Feeler
Judger/Perceiver
Sensing/Intuition
Calm/Excitable
Timid/Outgoing
Left Brain/Right Brain
Pessimist/Optimist/Realist
Motivated/Unmotivated
Controlled/Impulsive
Humble/Egotistical
Polite/Rude
A-B-O
Prioritizes/Procrastinates
Indoors/Outdoors
Efficient/Inefficient
Agile/Clumsy/Strong
Fight/Flight
Mischievous/Serious
Mature/Immature
Lazy/Hardworking
Predator/Prey
Common-Sense/Book-smarts
Private/TMI

Childish/Mature
Kind/Cruel/Uncaring
Laidback/High-strung
Cautious/Reckless
Leader/Follower
Loyal/Disloyal
Suspicious/Trusting
Mouth-filter/No-mouth-filter
Patient/Impatient
Intelligent/Average/Dumb-as-a-rock
Professional/Unprofessional
Formal/Informal
Quiet/Loud
Dominant/Submissive
Early/Late/On-Time
Athletic/Sedentary
Frivolous/Conservative
Routine/Spontaneity
Competitive/Passive
Self-blame/Blames-others
Logical/Emotional
Dedicated/Gives up
Flash Decisions/Contemplates
Wise/Foolish
Stubborn/Docile

Honest/Dishonest
Decisive/Indecisive
Forgiving/Grudges
Generous/Stingy
Warm/Cold
Grounded/Flighty
Reliable/Unreliable
Open/Secretive
Direct/Cautious/Daredevil
Dependent/Independent
Watcher/Participant
Night/Day
City/Country
Words/Fists
Neat/Messy
Focused/Distracted
Imaginative/Academic
Frugal/Wasteful
Flexible/Inflexible
Sweet/Sour/Bitter
Organized/Disorganized
Calm/Hot-tempered
Close/Long/Middle
Listens/Bullheaded
Generous/Selfish

Motivations: Wants or Needs: these often conflict.

_____
_____
_____
_____

What conflicts stand in the way?

_____
_____
_____

Notes:

_____
_____
_____
_____
_____

Story:	Role: MC, 2nd MC, 3rd MC, protagonist, antagonist, love interest, side kick, hapless bystander, other:
Book:	
Series:	Archetype: Tip: people have multiple facets. We don't pop out of molds.
Genre:	Primary Antagonist:

Name:
Tip: vary in first letter and length to limit confusion.

Age:

Eye Color:

Meaning:

DOB:

Hair Color:

Alias:

Height:

Hair Type:

Title:

Weight:

Hair Style:

Gender:

Build:

Skin Color:

Sexuality:

Blood Type:

Skin Tone:

Species:

Dominant Hand:

Voice:

Race:
Heritage born with.

Ethnicity:
Ethnicity is learned cultural behaviors.

Accent:
Tip: use with light touch.

Relationship Status:

Financial Status:

Social Class:

Identifying Features: injuries, scars, prosthetic, birthmarks, freckles, piercings, tattoos, alien features, biotech, scales, fangs, horns, ears, glasses, contacts, dimples, etc

Likes/Dislikes, Comforts/Fears, Strength/Weakness, Habits/Ticks

Character Traits

Tip: We are each a messy conflicted ball of contradictions. How can their own traits clash and force them to choose between two parts of themselves?

Introvert/Extrovert
Sarcastic/Quiet
Thinker/Feeler
Judger/Perceiver
Sensing/Intuition
Calm/Excitable
Timid/Outgoing
Left Brain/Right Brain
Pessimist/Optimist/Realist
Motivated/Unmotivated
Controlled/Impulsive
Humble/Egotistical
Polite/Rude
A-B-O
Prioritizes/Procrastinates
Indoors/Outdoors
Efficient/Inefficient
Agile/Clumsy/Strong
Fight/Flight
Mischievous/Serious
Mature/Immature
Lazy/Hardworking
Predator/Prey
Common-Sense/Book-smarts
Private/TMI

Childish/Mature
Kind/Cruel/Uncaring
Laidback/High-strung
Cautious/Reckless
Leader/Follower
Loyal/Disloyal
Suspicious/Trusting
Mouth-filter/No-mouth-filter
Patient/Impatient
Intelligent/Average/Dumb-as-a-rock
Professional/Unprofessional
Formal/Informal
Quiet/Loud
Dominant/Submissive
Early/Late/On-Time
Athletic/Sedentary
Frivolous/Conservative
Routine/Spontaneity
Competitive/Passive
Self-blame/Blames-others
Logical/Emotional
Dedicated/Gives up
Flash Decisions/Contemplates
Wise/Foolish
Stubborn/Docile

Honest/Dishonest
Decisive/Indecisive
Forgiving/Grudges
Generous/Stingy
Warm/Cold
Grounded/Flighty
Reliable/Unreliable
Open/Secretive
Direct/Cautious/Daredevil
Dependent/Independent
Watcher/Participant
Night/Day
City/Country
Words/Fists
Neat/Messy
Focused/Distracted
Imaginative/Academic
Frugal/Wasteful
Flexible/Inflexible
Sweet/Sour/Bitter
Organized/Disorganized
Calm/Hot-tempered
Close/Long/Middle
Listens/Bullheaded
Generous/Selfish

Motivations: Wants or Needs: these often conflict.

_____
_____
_____
_____

What conflicts stand in the way?

_____
_____
_____

Notes:

_____
_____
_____
_____
_____

Story:	Role: MC, 2nd MC, 3rd MC, protagonist, antagonist, love interest, side kick, hapless bystander, other:
Book:	
Series:	Archetype: Tip: people have multiple facets. We don't pop out of molds.
Genre:	Primary Antagonist:

Name:
Tip: vary in first letter and length to limit confusion.

Age:

Eye Color:

Meaning:

DOB:

Hair Color:

Alias:

Height:

Hair Type:

Title:

Weight:

Hair Style:

Gender:

Build:

Skin Color:

Sexuality:

Blood Type:

Skin Tone:

Species:

Dominant Hand:

Voice:

Race:

Heritage born with.

Ethnicity:
Ethnicity is learned cultural behaviors.

Accent:
Tip: use with light touch.

Relationship Status:

Financial Status:

Social Class:

Identifying Features: injuries, scars, prosthetic, birthmarks, freckles, piercings, tattoos, alien features, biotech, scales, fangs, horns, ears, glasses, contacts, dimples, etc

Likes/Dislikes, Comforts/Fears, Strength/Weakness, Habits/Ticks

Character Traits

Tip: We are each a messy conflicted ball of contradictions. How can their own traits clash and force them to choose between two parts of themselves?

Introvert/Extrovert
Sarcastic/Quiet
Thinker/Feeler
Judger/Perceiver
Sensing/Intuition
Calm/Excitable
Timid/Outgoing
Left Brain/Right Brain
Pessimist/Optimist/Realist
Motivated/Unmotivated
Controlled/Impulsive
Humble/Egotistical
Polite/Rude
A-B-O
Prioritizes/Procrastinates
Indoors/Outdoors
Efficient/Inefficient
Agile/Clumsy/Strong
Fight/Flight
Mischievous/Serious
Mature/Immature
Lazy/Hardworking
Predator/Prey
Common-Sense/Book-smarts
Private/TMI

Childish/Mature
Kind/Cruel/Uncaring
Laidback/High-strung
Cautious/Reckless
Leader/Follower
Loyal/Disloyal
Suspicious/Trusting
Mouth-filter/No-mouth-filter
Patient/Impatient
Intelligent/Average/Dumb-as-a-rock
Professional/Unprofessional
Formal/Informal
Quiet/Loud
Dominant/Submissive
Early/Late/On-Time
Athletic/Sedentary
Frivolous/Conservative
Routine/Spontaneity
Competitive/Passive
Self-blame/Blames-others
Logical/Emotional
Dedicated/Gives up
Flash Decisions/Contemplates
Wise/Foolish
Stubborn/Docile

Honest/Dishonest
Decisive/Indecisive
Forgiving/Grudges
Generous/Stingy
Warm/Cold
Grounded/Flighty
Reliable/Unreliable
Open/Secretive
Direct/Cautious/Daredevil
Dependent/Independent
Watcher/Participant
Night/Day
City/Country
Words/Fists
Neat/Messy
Focused/Distracted
Imaginative/Academic
Frugal/Wasteful
Flexible/Inflexible
Sweet/Sour/Bitter
Organized/Disorganized
Calm/Hot-tempered
Close/Long/Middle
Listens/Bullheaded
Generous/Selfish

Motivations: Wants or Needs: these often conflict.

_____
_____
_____
_____

What conflicts stand in the way?

_____
_____
_____

Notes:

_____
_____
_____
_____
_____

Story:	Role: MC, 2nd MC, 3rd MC, protagonist, antagonist, love interest, side kick, hapless bystander, other:
Book:	
Series:	Archetype: Tip: people have multiple facets. We don't pop out of molds.
Genre:	Primary Antagonist:

Name:
Tip: vary in first letter and length to limit confusion.

Age:

Eye Color:

Meaning:

DOB:

Hair Color:

Alias:

Height:

Hair Type:

Title:

Weight:

Hair Style:

Gender:

Build:

Skin Color:

Sexuality:

Blood Type:

Skin Tone:

Species:

Dominant Hand:

Voice:

Race:

Heritage born with.

Ethnicity:
Ethnicity is learned cultural behaviors.

Accent:
Tip: use with light touch.

Relationship Status:

Financial Status:

Social Class:

Identifying Features: injuries, scars, prosthetic, birthmarks, freckles, piercings, tattoos, alien features, biotech, scales, fangs, horns, ears, glasses, contacts, dimples, etc

Likes/Dislikes, Comforts/Fears, Strength/Weakness, Habits/Ticks

Character Traits

Tip: We are each a messy conflicted ball of contradictions. How can their own traits clash and force them to choose between two parts of themselves?

Introvert/Extrovert	Childish/Mature	Honest/Dishonest
Sarcastic/Quiet	Kind/Cruel/Uncaring	Decisive/Indecisive
Thinker/Feeler	Laidback/High-strung	Forgiving/Grudges
Judger/Perceiver	Cautious/Reckless	Generous/Stingy
Sensing/Intuition	Leader/Follower	Warm/Cold
Calm/Excitable	Loyal/Disloyal	Grounded/Flighty
Timid/Outgoing	Suspicious/Trusting	Reliable/Unreliable
Left Brain/Right Brain	Mouth-filter/No-mouth-filter	Open/Secretive
Pessimist/Optimist/Realist	Patient/Impatient	Direct/Cautious/Daredevil
Motivated/Unmotivated	Intelligent/Average/Dumb-as-a-rock	Dependent/Independent
Controlled/Impulsive		Watcher/Participant
Humble/Egotistical	Professional/Unprofessional	Night/Day
Polite/Rude	Formal/Informal	City/Country
A-B-O	Quiet/Loud	Words/Fists
Prioritizes/Procrastinates	Dominant/Submissive	Neat/Messy
Indoors/Outdoors	Early/Late/On-Time	Focused/Distracted
Efficient/Inefficient	Athletic/Sedentary	Imaginative/Academic
Agile/Clumsy/Strong	Frivolous/Conservative	Frugal/Wasteful
Fight/Flight	Routine/Spontaneity	Flexible/Inflexible
Mischievous/Serious	Competitive/Passive	Sweet/Sour/Bitter
Mature/Immature	Self-blame/Blames-others	Organized/Disorganized
Lazy/Hardworking	Logical/Emotional	Calm/Hot-tempered
Predator/Prey	Dedicated/Gives up	Close/Long/Middle
Common-Sense/Book-smarts	Flash Decisions/Contemplates	Listens/Bullheaded
	Wise/Foolish	Generous/Selfish
Private/TMI	Stubborn/Docile	

Motivations: Wants or Needs: these often conflict.

_____
_____
_____
_____

What conflicts stand in the way?

_____
_____
_____

Notes:

_____
_____
_____
_____
_____

Story:	Role: MC, 2nd MC, 3rd MC, protagonist, antagonist, love interest, side kick, hapless bystander, other:
Book:	
Series:	Archetype: Tip: people have multiple facets. We don't pop out of molds.
Genre:	Primary Antagonist:

Name:
Tip: vary in first letter and length to limit confusion.

Age:

Eye Color:

Meaning:

DOB:

Hair Color:

Alias:

Height:

Hair Type:

Title:

Weight:

Hair Style:

Gender:

Build:

Skin Color:

Sexuality:

Blood Type:

Skin Tone:

Species:

Dominant Hand:

Voice:

Race:
Heritage born with.

Ethnicity:
Ethnicity is learned cultural behaviors.

Accent:
Tip: use with light touch.

Relationship Status:

Financial Status:

Social Class:

Identifying Features: injuries, scars, prosthetic, birthmarks, freckles, piercings, tattoos, alien features, biotech, scales, fangs, horns, ears, glasses, contacts, dimples, etc

Likes/Dislikes, Comforts/Fears, Strength/Weakness, Habits/Ticks

Character Traits

Tip: We are each a messy conflicted ball of contradictions. How can their own traits clash and force them to choose between two parts of themselves?

Introvert/Extrovert
Sarcastic/Quiet
Thinker/Feeler
Judger/Perceiver
Sensing/Intuition
Calm/Excitable
Timid/Outgoing
Left Brain/Right Brain
Pessimist/Optimist/Realist
Motivated/Unmotivated
Controlled/Impulsive
Humble/Egotistical
Polite/Rude
A-B-O
Prioritizes/Procrastinates
Indoors/Outdoors
Efficient/Inefficient
Agile/Clumsy/Strong
Fight/Flight
Mischievous/Serious
Mature/Immature
Lazy/Hardworking
Predator/Prey
Common-Sense/Book-smarts
Private/TMI

Childish/Mature
Kind/Cruel/Uncaring
Laidback/High-strung
Cautious/Reckless
Leader/Follower
Loyal/Disloyal
Suspicious/Trusting
Mouth-filter/No-mouth-filter
Patient/Impatient
Intelligent/Average/Dumb-as-a-rock
Professional/Unprofessional
Formal/Informal
Quiet/Loud
Dominant/Submissive
Early/Late/On-Time
Athletic/Sedentary
Frivolous/Conservative
Routine/Spontaneity
Competitive/Passive
Self-blame/Blames-others
Logical/Emotional
Dedicated/Gives up
Flash Decisions/Contemplates
Wise/Foolish
Stubborn/Docile

Honest/Dishonest
Decisive/Indecisive
Forgiving/Grudges
Generous/Stingy
Warm/Cold
Grounded/Flighty
Reliable/Unreliable
Open/Secretive
Direct/Cautious/Daredevil
Dependent/Independent
Watcher/Participant
Night/Day
City/Country
Words/Fists
Neat/Messy
Focused/Distracted
Imaginative/Academic
Frugal/Wasteful
Flexible/Inflexible
Sweet/Sour/Bitter
Organized/Disorganized
Calm/Hot-tempered
Close/Long/Middle
Listens/Bullheaded
Generous/Selfish

Motivations: Wants or Needs: these often conflict.

_____
_____
_____
_____

What conflicts stand in the way?

_____
_____
_____

Notes:

_____
_____
_____
_____
_____

Story:	Role: MC, 2nd MC, 3rd MC, protagonist, antagonist, love interest, side kick, hapless bystander, other:
Book:	
Series:	Archetype: Tip: people have multiple facets. We don't pop out of molds.
Genre:	Primary Antagonist:

Name:
Tip: vary in first letter and length to limit confusion.

Age:

Eye Color:

Meaning:

DOB:

Hair Color:

Alias:

Height:

Hair Type:

Title:

Weight:

Hair Style:

Gender:

Build:

Skin Color:

Sexuality:

Blood Type:

Skin Tone:

Species:

Dominant Hand:

Voice:

Race:

Heritage born with.

Ethnicity:
Ethnicity is learned cultural behaviors.

Accent:
Tip: use with light touch.

Relationship Status:

Financial Status:

Social Class:

Identifying Features: injuries, scars, prosthetic, birthmarks, freckles, piercings, tattoos, alien features, biotech, scales, fangs, horns, ears, glasses, contacts, dimples, etc

Likes/Dislikes, Comforts/Fears, Strength/Weakness, Habits/Ticks

Character Traits

Tip: We are each a messy conflicted ball of contradictions. How can their own traits clash and force them to choose between two parts of themselves?

Introvert/Extrovert
Sarcastic/Quiet
Thinker/Feeler
Judger/Perceiver
Sensing/Intuition
Calm/Excitable
Timid/Outgoing
Left Brain/Right Brain
Pessimist/Optimist/Realist
Motivated/Unmotivated
Controlled/Impulsive
Humble/Egotistical
Polite/Rude
A-B-O
Prioritizes/Procrastinates
Indoors/Outdoors
Efficient/Inefficient
Agile/Clumsy/Strong
Fight/Flight
Mischievous/Serious
Mature/Immature
Lazy/Hardworking
Predator/Prey
Common-Sense/Book-smarts
Private/TMI

Childish/Mature
Kind/Cruel/Uncaring
Laidback/High-strung
Cautious/Reckless
Leader/Follower
Loyal/Disloyal
Suspicious/Trusting
Mouth-filter/No-mouth-filter
Patient/Impatient
Intelligent/Average/Dumb-as-a-rock
Professional/Unprofessional
Formal/Informal
Quiet/Loud
Dominant/Submissive
Early/Late/On-Time
Athletic/Sedentary
Frivolous/Conservative
Routine/Spontaneity
Competitive/Passive
Self-blame/Blames-others
Logical/Emotional
Dedicated/Gives up
Flash Decisions/Contemplates
Wise/Foolish
Stubborn/Docile

Honest/Dishonest
Decisive/Indecisive
Forgiving/Grudges
Generous/Stingy
Warm/Cold
Grounded/Flighty
Reliable/Unreliable
Open/Secretive
Direct/Cautious/Daredevil
Dependent/Independent
Watcher/Participant
Night/Day
City/Country
Words/Fists
Neat/Messy
Focused/Distracted
Imaginative/Academic
Frugal/Wasteful
Flexible/Inflexible
Sweet/Sour/Bitter
Organized/Disorganized
Calm/Hot-tempered
Close/Long/Middle
Listens/Bullheaded
Generous/Selfish

Motivations: Wants or Needs: these often conflict.

_____
_____
_____
_____

What conflicts stand in the way?

_____
_____
_____

Notes:

_____
_____
_____
_____
_____

Story:	Role: MC, 2nd MC, 3rd MC, protagonist, antagonist, love interest, side kick, hapless bystander, other:
Book:	
Series:	Archetype: Tip: people have multiple facets. We don't pop out of molds.
Genre:	Primary Antagonist:

Name:
Tip: vary in first letter and length to limit confusion.

Age:

Eye Color:

Meaning:

DOB:

Hair Color:

Alias:

Height:

Hair Type:

Title:

Weight:

Hair Style:

Gender:

Build:

Skin Color:

Sexuality:

Blood Type:

Skin Tone:

Species:

Dominant Hand:

Voice:

Race:
Heritage born with.

Ethnicity:
Ethnicity is learned cultural behaviors.

Accent:
Tip: use with light touch.

Relationship Status:

Financial Status:

Social Class:

Identifying Features: injuries, scars, prosthetic, birthmarks, freckles, piercings, tattoos, alien features, biotech, scales, fangs, horns, ears, glasses, contacts, dimples, etc

Likes/Dislikes, Comforts/Fears, Strength/Weakness, Habits/Ticks

Character Traits

Tip: We are each a messy conflicted ball of contradictions. How can their own traits clash and force them to choose between two parts of themselves?

Introvert/Extrovert	Childish/Mature	Honest/Dishonest
Sarcastic/Quiet	Kind/Cruel/Uncaring	Decisive/Indecisive
Thinker/Feeler	Laidback/High-strung	Forgiving/Grudges
Judger/Perceiver	Cautious/Reckless	Generous/Stingy
Sensing/Intuition	Leader/Follower	Warm/Cold
Calm/Excitable	Loyal/Disloyal	Grounded/Flighty
Timid/Outgoing	Suspicious/Trusting	Reliable/Unreliable
Left Brain/Right Brain	Mouth-filter/No-mouth-filter	Open/Secretive
Pessimist/Optimist/Realist	Patient/Impatient	Direct/Cautious/Daredevil
Motivated/Unmotivated	Intelligent/Average/Dumb-as-	Dependent/Independent
Controlled/Impulsive	a-rock	Watcher/Participant
Humble/Egotistical	Professional/Unprofessional	Night/Day
Polite/Rude	Formal/Informal	City/Country
A-B-O	Quiet/Loud	Words/Fists
Prioritizes/Procrastinates	Dominant/Submissive	Neat/Messy
Indoors/Outdoors	Early/Late/On-Time	Focused/Distracted
Efficient/Inefficient	Athletic/Sedentary	Imaginative/Academic
Agile/Clumsy/Strong	Frivolous/Conservative	Frugal/Wasteful
Fight/Flight	Routine/Spontaneity	Flexible/Inflexible
Mischievous/Serious	Competitive/Passive	Sweet/Sour/Bitter
Mature/Immature	Self-blame/Blames-others	Organized/Disorganized
Lazy/Hardworking	Logical/Emotional	Calm/Hot-tempered
Predator/Prey	Dedicated/Gives up	Close/Long/Middle
Common-Sense/Book-	Flash Decisions/Contemplates	Listens/Bullheaded
smarts	Wise/Foolish	Generous/Selfish
Private/TMI	Stubborn/Docile	

Motivations: Wants or Needs: these often conflict.

_____
_____
_____
_____

What conflicts stand in the way?

_____
_____
_____

Notes:

_____
_____
_____
_____
_____

Story:	Role: MC, 2nd MC, 3rd MC, protagonist, antagonist, love interest, side kick, hapless bystander, other:
Book:	
Series:	Archetype: Tip: people have multiple facets. We don't pop out of molds.
Genre:	Primary Antagonist:

Name:
Tip: vary in first letter and length to limit confusion.

Age:

Eye Color:

Meaning:

DOB:

Hair Color:

Alias:

Height:

Hair Type:

Title:

Weight:

Hair Style:

Gender:

Build:

Skin Color:

Sexuality:

Blood Type:

Skin Tone:

Species:

Dominant Hand:

Voice:

Race:
Heritage born with.

Ethnicity:
Ethnicity is learned cultural behaviors.

Accent:
Tip: use with light touch.

Relationship Status:

Financial Status:

Social Class:

Identifying Features: injuries, scars, prosthetic, birthmarks, freckles, piercings, tattoos, alien features, biotech, scales, fangs, horns, ears, glasses, contacts, dimples, etc

Likes/Dislikes, Comforts/Fears, Strength/Weakness, Habits/Ticks

Character Traits

Tip: We are each a messy conflicted ball of contradictions. How can their own traits clash and force them to choose between two parts of themselves?

Introvert/Extrovert	Childish/Mature	Honest/Dishonest
Sarcastic/Quiet	Kind/Cruel/Uncaring	Decisive/Indecisive
Thinker/Feeler	Laidback/High-strung	Forgiving/Grudges
Judger/Perceiver	Cautious/Reckless	Generous/Stingy
Sensing/Intuition	Leader/Follower	Warm/Cold
Calm/Excitable	Loyal/Disloyal	Grounded/Flighty
Timid/Outgoing	Suspicious/Trusting	Reliable/Unreliable
Left Brain/Right Brain	Mouth-filter/No-mouth-filter	Open/Secretive
Pessimist/Optimist/Realist	Patient/Impatient	Direct/Cautious/Daredevil
Motivated/Unmotivated	Intelligent/Average/Dumb-as-	Dependent/Independent
Controlled/Impulsive	a-rock	Watcher/Participant
Humble/Egotistical	Professional/Unprofessional	Night/Day
Polite/Rude	Formal/Informal	City/Country
A-B-O	Quiet/Loud	Words/Fists
Prioritizes/Procrastinates	Dominant/Submissive	Neat/Messy
Indoors/Outdoors	Early/Late/On-Time	Focused/Distracted
Efficient/Inefficient	Athletic/Sedentary	Imaginative/Academic
Agile/Clumsy/Strong	Frivolous/Conservative	Frugal/Wasteful
Fight/Flight	Routine/Spontaneity	Flexible/Inflexible
Mischievous/Serious	Competitive/Passive	Sweet/Sour/Bitter
Mature/Immature	Self-blame/Blames-others	Organized/Disorganized
Lazy/Hardworking	Logical/Emotional	Calm/Hot-tempered
Predator/Prey	Dedicated/Gives up	Close/Long/Middle
Common-Sense/Book-	Flash Decisions/Contemplates	Listens/Bullheaded
smarts	Wise/Foolish	Generous/Selfish
Private/TMI	Stubborn/Docile	

Motivations: Wants or Needs: these often conflict.

_____
_____
_____
_____

What conflicts stand in the way?

_____
_____
_____

Notes:

_____
_____
_____
_____
_____

Story:	Role: MC, 2nd MC, 3rd MC, protagonist, antagonist, love interest, side kick, hapless bystander, other:
Book:	
Series:	Archetype: Tip: people have multiple facets. We don't pop out of molds.
Genre:	Primary Antagonist:

Name:
Tip: vary in first letter and length to limit confusion.

Age:

Eye Color:

Meaning:

DOB:

Hair Color:

Alias:

Height:

Hair Type:

Title:

Weight:

Hair Style:

Gender:

Build:

Skin Color:

Sexuality:

Blood Type:

Skin Tone:

Species:

Dominant Hand:

Voice:

Race:

Heritage born with.

Ethnicity:
Ethnicity is learned cultural behaviors.

Accent:
Tip: use with light touch.

Relationship Status:

Financial Status:

Social Class:

Identifying Features: injuries, scars, prosthetic, birthmarks, freckles, piercings, tattoos, alien features, biotech, scales, fangs, horns, ears, glasses, contacts, dimples, etc

Likes/Dislikes, Comforts/Fears, Strength/Weakness, Habits/Ticks

Character Traits

Tip: We are each a messy conflicted ball of contradictions. How can their own traits clash and force them to choose between two parts of themselves?

Introvert/Extrovert
Sarcastic/Quiet
Thinker/Feeler
Judger/Perceiver
Sensing/Intuition
Calm/Excitable
Timid/Outgoing
Left Brain/Right Brain
Pessimist/Optimist/Realist
Motivated/Unmotivated
Controlled/Impulsive
Humble/Egotistical
Polite/Rude
A-B-O
Prioritizes/Procrastinates
Indoors/Outdoors
Efficient/Inefficient
Agile/Clumsy/Strong
Fight/Flight
Mischievous/Serious
Mature/Immature
Lazy/Hardworking
Predator/Prey
Common-Sense/Book-smarts
Private/TMI

Childish/Mature
Kind/Cruel/Uncaring
Laidback/High-strung
Cautious/Reckless
Leader/Follower
Loyal/Disloyal
Suspicious/Trusting
Mouth-filter/No-mouth-filter
Patient/Impatient
Intelligent/Average/Dumb-as-a-rock
Professional/Unprofessional
Formal/Informal
Quiet/Loud
Dominant/Submissive
Early/Late/On-Time
Athletic/Sedentary
Frivolous/Conservative
Routine/Spontaneity
Competitive/Passive
Self-blame/Blames-others
Logical/Emotional
Dedicated/Gives up
Flash Decisions/Contemplates
Wise/Foolish
Stubborn/Docile

Honest/Dishonest
Decisive/Indecisive
Forgiving/Grudges
Generous/Stingy
Warm/Cold
Grounded/Flighty
Reliable/Unreliable
Open/Secretive
Direct/Cautious/Daredevil
Dependent/Independent
Watcher/Participant
Night/Day
City/Country
Words/Fists
Neat/Messy
Focused/Distracted
Imaginative/Academic
Frugal/Wasteful
Flexible/Inflexible
Sweet/Sour/Bitter
Organized/Disorganized
Calm/Hot-tempered
Close/Long/Middle
Listens/Bullheaded
Generous/Selfish

Motivations: Wants or Needs: these often conflict.

_____
_____
_____
_____

What conflicts stand in the way?

_____
_____
_____

Notes:

_____
_____
_____
_____
_____

Story:	Role: MC, 2nd MC, 3rd MC, protagonist, antagonist, love interest, side kick, hapless bystander, other:
Book:	
Series:	Archetype: Tip: people have multiple facets. We don't pop out of molds.
Genre:	Primary Antagonist:

Name:
Tip: vary in first letter and length to limit confusion.

Age:

Eye Color:

Meaning:

DOB:

Hair Color:

Alias:

Height:

Hair Type:

Title:

Weight:

Hair Style:

Gender:

Build:

Skin Color:

Sexuality:

Blood Type:

Skin Tone:

Species:

Dominant Hand:

Voice:

Race:
Heritage born with.

Ethnicity:
Ethnicity is learned cultural behaviors.

Accent:
Tip: use with light touch.

Relationship Status:

Financial Status:

Social Class:

Identifying Features: injuries, scars, prosthetic, birthmarks, freckles, piercings, tattoos, alien features, biotech, scales, fangs, horns, ears, glasses, contacts, dimples, etc

Likes/Dislikes, Comforts/Fears, Strength/Weakness, Habits/Ticks

Character Traits

Tip: We are each a messy conflicted ball of contradictions. How can their own traits clash and force them to choose between two parts of themselves?

Introvert/Extrovert
Sarcastic/Quiet
Thinker/Feeler
Judger/Perceiver
Sensing/Intuition
Calm/Excitable
Timid/Outgoing
Left Brain/Right Brain
Pessimist/Optimist/Realist
Motivated/Unmotivated
Controlled/Impulsive
Humble/Egotistical
Polite/Rude
A-B-O
Prioritizes/Procrastinates
Indoors/Outdoors
Efficient/Inefficient
Agile/Clumsy/Strong
Fight/Flight
Mischievous/Serious
Mature/Immature
Lazy/Hardworking
Predator/Prey
Common-Sense/Book-smarts
Private/TMI

Childish/Mature
Kind/Cruel/Uncaring
Laidback/High-strung
Cautious/Reckless
Leader/Follower
Loyal/Disloyal
Suspicious/Trusting
Mouth-filter/No-mouth-filter
Patient/Impatient
Intelligent/Average/Dumb-as-a-rock
Professional/Unprofessional
Formal/Informal
Quiet/Loud
Dominant/Submissive
Early/Late/On-Time
Athletic/Sedentary
Frivolous/Conservative
Routine/Spontaneity
Competitive/Passive
Self-blame/Blames-others
Logical/Emotional
Dedicated/Gives up
Flash Decisions/Contemplates
Wise/Foolish
Stubborn/Docile

Honest/Dishonest
Decisive/Indecisive
Forgiving/Grudges
Generous/Stingy
Warm/Cold
Grounded/Flighty
Reliable/Unreliable
Open/Secretive
Direct/Cautious/Daredevil
Dependent/Independent
Watcher/Participant
Night/Day
City/Country
Words/Fists
Neat/Messy
Focused/Distracted
Imaginative/Academic
Frugal/Wasteful
Flexible/Inflexible
Sweet/Sour/Bitter
Organized/Disorganized
Calm/Hot-tempered
Close/Long/Middle
Listens/Bullheaded
Generous/Selfish

Motivations: Wants or Needs: these often conflict.

_____
_____
_____
_____

What conflicts stand in the way?

_____
_____
_____

Notes:

_____
_____
_____
_____
_____

Story:	Role: MC, 2nd MC, 3rd MC, protagonist, antagonist, love interest, side kick, hapless bystander, other:
Book:	
Series:	Archetype: Tip: people have multiple facets. We don't pop out of molds.
Genre:	Primary Antagonist:

Name:
Tip: vary in first letter and length to limit confusion.

Age:

Eye Color:

Meaning:

DOB:

Hair Color:

Alias:

Height:

Hair Type:

Title:

Weight:

Hair Style:

Gender:

Build:

Skin Color:

Sexuality:

Blood Type:

Skin Tone:

Species:

Dominant Hand:

Voice:

Race:

Heritage born with.

Ethnicity:

Ethnicity is learned cultural behaviors.

Accent:

Tip: use with light touch.

Relationship Status:

Financial Status:

Social Class:

Identifying Features: injuries, scars, prosthetic, birthmarks, freckles, piercings, tattoos, alien features, biotech, scales, fangs, horns, ears, glasses, contacts, dimples, etc

Likes/Dislikes, Comforts/Fears, Strength/Weakness, Habits/Ticks

Character Traits

Tip: We are each a messy conflicted ball of contradictions. How can their own traits clash and force them to choose between two parts of themselves?

Introvert/Extrovert
Sarcastic/Quiet
Thinker/Feeler
Judger/Perceiver
Sensing/Intuition
Calm/Excitable
Timid/Outgoing
Left Brain/Right Brain
Pessimist/Optimist/Realist
Motivated/Unmotivated
Controlled/Impulsive
Humble/Egotistical
Polite/Rude
A-B-O
Prioritizes/Procrastinates
Indoors/Outdoors
Efficient/Inefficient
Agile/Clumsy/Strong
Fight/Flight
Mischievous/Serious
Mature/Immature
Lazy/Hardworking
Predator/Prey
Common-Sense/Book-smarts
Private/TMI

Childish/Mature
Kind/Cruel/Uncaring
Laidback/High-strung
Cautious/Reckless
Leader/Follower
Loyal/Disloyal
Suspicious/Trusting
Mouth-filter/No-mouth-filter
Patient/Impatient
Intelligent/Average/Dumb-as-a-rock
Professional/Unprofessional
Formal/Informal
Quiet/Loud
Dominant/Submissive
Early/Late/On-Time
Athletic/Sedentary
Frivolous/Conservative
Routine/Spontaneity
Competitive/Passive
Self-blame/Blames-others
Logical/Emotional
Dedicated/Gives up
Flash Decisions/Contemplates
Wise/Foolish
Stubborn/Docile

Honest/Dishonest
Decisive/Indecisive
Forgiving/Grudges
Generous/Stingy
Warm/Cold
Grounded/Flighty
Reliable/Unreliable
Open/Secretive
Direct/Cautious/Daredevil
Dependent/Independent
Watcher/Participant
Night/Day
City/Country
Words/Fists
Neat/Messy
Focused/Distracted
Imaginative/Academic
Frugal/Wasteful
Flexible/Inflexible
Sweet/Sour/Bitter
Organized/Disorganized
Calm/Hot-tempered
Close/Long/Middle
Listens/Bullheaded
Generous/Selfish

Motivations: Wants or Needs: these often conflict.

_____
_____
_____
_____

What conflicts stand in the way?

_____
_____
_____

Notes:

_____
_____
_____
_____
_____

Made in United States
Troutdale, OR
04/28/2025